All About Perennials

Created and designed by
the editorial staff of
ORTHO BOOKS

Project Manager
Cynthia Putnam

Manuscript Editor
Sara Godwin

Writers
A. Cort Sinnes
Larry Hodgson

Consultant
Allen Paterson

Photography Editor
Judy Mason

Designer
Gary Hespenheide

Ortho Books

Publisher
Richard E. Pile, Jr.

Editorial Director
Christine Jordan

Production Director
Ernie S. Tasaki

Managing Editors
Robert J. Beckstrom
Michael D. Smith
Sally W. Smith

System Manager
Linda M. Bouchard

Marketing Specialist
Daniel Stage

Sales Manager
Thomas J. Leahy

Distribution Specialist
Barbara F. Steadham

Technical Consultant
J. A. Crozier, Jr., Ph.D.

Address all inquiries to:
Ortho Books
Box 5006
San Ramon, CA 94583-0906

5	6	7	8	9
94	95	96	97	

ISBN 0-89721-247-9
Library of Congress Catalog Card
Number 92-70588

THE SOLARIS GROUP
2527 Camino Ramon
San Ramon, CA 94583-0906

Acknowledgments

Copy Chief
Melinda E. Levine

Editorial Coordinator
Cass Dempsey

Copyeditor
Rebecca Pepper

Proofreader
Deborah Bruner

Indexer
Trisha Feuerstein

Composition by
Nancy Patton Wilson

Editorial Assistant
Laurie A. Steele

Associate Editor
Sara Shopkow

Production by
Studio 165

Separations by
Color Tech Corp.

Lithographed in the USA by
Webcrafters, Inc.

Photographers
Names of photographers are followed by the page numbers on which their work appears. R=right, C=center, L=left, T=top, B=bottom.

R. & D. Aitkenhead, Positive Images: 57R
Margarite Bradley, Positive Images: 39
Gay Bumgarner, Photo/Nats: 34
Karen Bussolini, Positive Images: 7T, 11, 44
Kristie Callan: 47TL, 47TR, 47CL, 47CR, 47BL
David Cavagnaro: 31, 68R, 74R, 76R, 77BR, 79L, 95L, 96R, 98L, 105R, 107R
Jack Clark, COMSTOCK: 47BR
Josephine Coatsworth: 12, 25, 36, 37, back cover TL
Greg Crisci, Photo/Nats: 69R
Derek Fell: 69L, 70L, 81R, 97L, 104L, 104R
Jean Fogle, Photo/Nats: 98R
Jennifer Graylock, Photo/Nats: 88L
Margaret Hensel, Positive Images: 8, 22, 29, 30, 33, 42, 45, 61R, 70R, 75L, 93L, 102L, back cover BR
Jerry Howard, Positive Images: 4, 17, 50, 84L, 90L, 90R, 92R, 106L
Michael Landis: 64L
Peter Lindtner: 40, 52R, 54R, 58, 60R, 62C, 62R, 65L, 74L, 89L, 89R, 91L
Dorothy Long, Photo/Nats: 48
Arleen Lorrance, Positive Images: 73L
John Lynch, Photo/Nats: 62L
Michael McKinley: 26, 51R, 56L, 57L, 60L, 63R, 66L, 66R, 67, 80L, 80R, 81L, 82L, 83R, 84R, 85L, 85R, 87, 91R, 95R, 99L, 100L, 101L, 103L, 105L, back cover TR
James McNair: 55L
Ivan Masser, Positive Images: 73R
Ortho Information Services: 51L, 59L, 92L
Jerry & Joanne Pavia: 7B, 52L, 59R, 63L, 94R
Ann Reilly, Photo/Nats: 56R, 72R, 78L, 93R, 97R, 107L
Steven Still: 53L, 53R, 54L, 55R, 61L, 64R, 68L, 71L, 71R, 72L, 76L, 77TL, 77TR, 77BL, 78TR, 78BR, 79R, 82R, 83L, 86, 88R, 94L, 96L, 99R, 100R, 101R, 102R, 103R, 106R, back cover BL
David Stone, Photo/Nats: 65R, 75R
Michael Thompson, COMSTOCK: Front cover, title page, 43

Front Cover
Columbine (*Aquilegia*), larkspur (*Delphinium*), lilac (*Syringa*), and phlox (*Phlox*) are as attractive in a border together as they are in a bouquet.

Back Cover
Top left: Blue statice, several species of pink pelargoniums, and English ivy tumble merrily over the sides of a stone urn.

Top right: Yellow foxtail lilies give a strong vertical accent in a hot color perennial border of red poppies, red Maltese cross, and yellow yarrow.

Bottom left: Red common sneezeweed is effective when massed together.

Bottom right: A single 'Broadway' iris is spectacular.

Title Page
California poppies in bright yellow and orange bloom with blue forget-me-not to make a living bouquet.

All About Perennials

Favorites for All Time

Perennials are the flesh and bones of the garden, giving it both structure and shape. Because they come back faithfully year after year, they establish and reinforce the continuity of the garden's design. Their colors are consistent from year to year, making it possible to work out color schemes and effects that are particularly satisfying and spectacular. Their flowers provide, if a small pun can be forgiven, a perennial delight.

Many people find an old-fashioned appeal in perennial flowers. Some use them for long-term, low-maintenance color; others make collecting and growing perennials a lifelong hobby. Any way you look at them, perennials mean beauty and pleasure to the gardener.

For many people, perennials call up images of the kind of garden Grandma used to grow. In fact, many perennials are old-fashioned, having been the favorites of many generations of gardeners. They are also the favorites of many gardeners today, and for the same reasons as in the past: They are relatively easy to grow, they last from year to year, and they offer an abundance of flowers in an enormous array of colors and forms.

Black-eyed-susans (Rudbeckia) *provide a burst of summer color in this pretty perennial border.*

WHAT IS A PERENNIAL?

What distinguishes perennials from other plants? The best way to answer this question is to begin by comparing them with annuals and biennials.

Annuals complete their entire life cycle in a year or less. In most cases, annuals are planted from seed in the spring, flower and set seed during the summer and early fall, and are killed by the first hard frosts of winter.

Biennials take two years to complete their life cycle. When grown from seed, they produce leaves but no flowers the first year; the second year they flower, set seed, and die.

Perennials live more than two years. Many plants are perennial, including trees, shrubs, and bulbs. The word *perennial,* as it is commonly used and as it is used in this book, refers to herbaceous flowering plants. *Herbaceous* means that the stems are soft and fleshy rather than woody like those of shrubs and trees. (Bulbs are classified separately because of their method of storing food.)

Woody shrubs and trees survive winters because their stems and trunks resist extreme cold. Herbaceous perennials survive varying degrees of winter cold by virtue of roots that are stronger and more vigorous than those of annuals. The tops of perennials die down with the onset of cold, but the roots remain alive in a dormant state, sending forth new foliage and flowers each year when the weather warms. If the growing conditions are right, this pattern can continue for many years. Some long-lived perennials, such as peony, gasplant, bleedingheart, and plantain lily, have been known to outlive their owners.

The longevity of perennials gives the gardener some outstanding advantages. Their presence in the garden year after year saves the time, labor, and expense of replanting every spring. In addition, perennials provide an established framework around which seasonal garden effects can be planned and planted. This lends a valuable coherence to the garden from one year to the next.

Perennials have other advantages as well. Plants well adapted to your climate and planted in the right location will require very little attention. And since most perennials reproduce by sending out roots that generate new plants, they can provide you with vigorous stock ready for transplanting.

Most intriguing for many gardeners is the fact that perennials come in an amazing profusion of colors, shapes, and sizes. There are literally thousands of varieties available. This delightful diversity makes even the mere planning of a perennial garden an exciting and satisfying enterprise.

HOW TO USE THIS BOOK

This is both an idea book and a book of basic information. It contains ideas for combining and using perennials in many ways. More importantly, it gives you the practical information you need to produce your own beautiful perennial garden.

If you are interested in planning a garden but are at a loss as to where to begin, read "Designing With Perennials," beginning on page 9. There you will find everything you need to know to plan a garden that pleases you, from how to use perennials as spot plantings to how to lay out formal or informal beds and borders. The chapter gives valuable advice on choosing colors and color combinations as well as solid guidelines on the trickiest aspect of perennial gardening: coordinating the blooming times of different perennials to achieve the effects you want. You will also find practical information on planting a mixed perennial border, a perennial cutting garden, and a perennial container garden.

To grow healthy and handsome perennials, see "From the Ground Up," on page 35. This chapter explains how to get the soil in good condition, where to find the best plants, and how to start perennials from seed. It also has all the essential information on fertilizing, watering, and mulching as well as pest and disease control.

The "Plant Selection Guide," starting on page 49, is an invaluable reference for both beginning and veteran gardeners. The guide lists more than a hundred different perennials commonly grown in the United States. Photographs of the flowers help you visualize your projected garden and help you identify the plants. The guide also provides detailed information on culture and potential problems and tells how to get the most flowers from each plant.

BEFORE YOU BEGIN

When you set out to create a beautiful garden, there are many practical matters to consider, especially in the vast world of perennials.

These include the design of the garden, where to find the perennials you want, and the details of how to grow those perennials successfully. In addition to providing that information, this book is meant to kindle an enthusiasm for gardening with perennials that goes beyond the strictly practical considerations.

Gardeners are among the most talented people on Earth when it comes to creating a beautiful environment. The transformation of a bare plot of ground into a garden filled with color, fragrance, the play of sunlight and shadow, and the sounds of bird song and falling water is almost magical.

Many of the photographs in this book have caught that magic. Do not hesitate to re-create, perhaps identically, some of the ideas presented on the pages that follow. They are meant to be an inspiration for anyone wanting to create a special magic in the garden.

The single clump of Siberian iris (Iris sibirica) *helps create the streamside illusion suggested by this dry stream bed of rounded rocks.*

This classic perennial border of larkspur, foxglove, and yellow sundrops bordered by pink and white cottage pinks is set off beautifully by a background of evergreens.

Designing With Perennials

Perennial flowering plants are extremely versatile. They are at home in any type of garden, from the formal perfection of a perennial border to the humblest of cottage gardens.

Perennials as a group are the most versatile plants in the landscape. There are perennials that thrive in every sort of soil from wet to dry and rich to poor and in every exposure from full sun to shade. Some perennials flourish alongside streams or in the dappled shade of trees; others grow happily in meadows or in problem areas such as hillsides, steep embankments, and rocky outcroppings.

If you have an established low-maintenance landscape of trees and shrubs and want to add some seasonal color to relieve the year-round monotony of the scene, perennials are the perfect way to do it without having to replant every year. Adding even a few perennials to a dull landscape can transform it into an attractive garden.

As versatile and effective as perennials are in difficult or unconventional situations, it is in the flower garden that they are truly outstanding. Year after year they can provide beautiful flowers and foliage over a long season, from early spring until late fall. They are solid, reliable plants, and the feeling of permanence and stability they bring to the garden in turn gives deep satisfaction and a welcome sense of security to every gardener.

It doesn't take much to create a striking effect with perennials; here, dark blue false-indigo (Baptisia australis) *and a lush white peony work well together.*

THE PERENNIAL BORDER

People have loved perennial gardening for centuries, so much so that it has developed, particularly in the form of the perennial border, into a genuine art. The border reached its peak of perfection at the turn of the century when Gertrude Jekyll, trained as an artist during the Impressionist period, created painterly effects in her famous borders. Her borders set the standards by which all perennial borders are judged, even now, some sixty years after her death. Her own color border at Munstead Wood was 200 feet long, 18 feet wide, and backed by a sandstone wall covered with climbing vines, which served as a backdrop for her herbaceous perennials. Jekyll was so serious about her gardening that much of the garden was laid out before the house was built.

The Cottage Garden

The best place to begin learning about garden design is with the type of garden that shows the least design of all: the cottage garden. The English cottage garden, using the same plants as its formal ornamental counterparts, was the forerunner of the most beautifully designed perennial beds and borders. Cottage gardens were the small dooryards of cottagers who worked on the grand estates. They grew foxglove and peonies, less for their flowers than for their medicinal uses, since the cottager's wife was often the only doctor the family knew. Cabbage and kale grew cheek-by-jowl with bugbane and feverfew, for the cottage garden provided not only medicine but food. And of course there were always some flowers grown "just for pretty." Whereas fashionable gardeners planted exotics from the New World in their gardens, the old-fashioned favorites remained in the cottage gardens. Gertrude Jekyll saw these charming, sturdy, reliable old favorites and used them to create her borders, bringing them once again into fashion.

Today cottage gardens are essentially the gardens of people who love plants for themselves and care little or nothing for the way they are organized. Plants are added to suit the taste and whim of the gardener. The guiding principle is to have close at hand all of those plants the gardener loves, without much regard for such rules as placing taller plants in back or leading up to bright colors with more subtle ones. The effect is likely to be kaleidoscopic, with an old climbing rose, a clump of daylilies, a mat of nasturtiums, a towering stand of hollyhocks, and spots of cottage pinks, basket-of-gold, speedwell, poppies, and other plants all growing wherever they were plunked, without much focus or forethought. These are gardens of surprises, where such accidents of nature as the encroaching of vigorous plants upon one another and the sudden appearance of plants the gardener doesn't recall planting are gratefully accepted. The true cottage garden has a wild and woolly look, but it is also a charming, engaging garden in which to lose oneself.

It may be that this casual approach to gardening and garden design appeals to you more than the idea of sitting down with graph paper and a ruler and laying out a plan. Why, then, should you bother learning anything about the techniques of design?

WHY DESIGN?

The simple fact is that gardens can have the same quantities of exactly the same plants, and some of these gardens will still be more attractive than others. In almost every case, the difference is that the most beautiful gardens are those with a strong underlying design or structure. The sense of order a plan provides is especially important in flower gardens. With flowering plants, the variations in sizes, shapes, colors, and textures make it possible to end up with a confused jumble, one that means less pleasure and more work. If the basic framework of the garden is strong, it will support almost any combination of plants and flowers easily, without horticultural chaos.

Unfortunately, beginning gardeners too often ignore the planning stage. Their gardens tend to grow randomly, by bits and pieces, and if some order does emerge, it is more by luck than conscious effort. In the long run, however, a much more beautiful garden results if you take the time to draw up some sort of overall plan. By the time your garden matures, this underlying design may not be as obvious as in the beginning, but the organization it provided will still be strongly felt.

PLANNING THE DESIGN

At the beginning of any truly successful garden, a thoughtful plan is devised and carried out. Such factors as the lawn size and shape, paths and walkways, shrub borders, hedges, trees, ornaments, and background fences and walls are all considered, individually and also as contributors to the final effect.

There are five basic steps to designing a perennial garden.

1. Determine the point from which the garden most often will be viewed.

2. Consider the shape and topography of your yard and decide which of the existing plants will remain where they are.

3. Choose a formal or an informal design.

4. Decide whether to have a bed or a border and choose an edging, and, for a border, a background.

5. Choose which plants to use.

Viewpoint and Topography

The first step in planning your garden should be determining the angle or location from which it will most often be viewed. If you plan to view your garden primarily from inside the house, locate it where it can be comfortably enjoyed through a favorite window. If you plan to spend a lot of time on a deck or patio, lay out the garden with that in mind.

Once you have determined the garden's location, the next step is to consider the shape and topography of your yard. This will help determine whether a formal or informal design would work best.

Formal or Informal?

If your yard is irregular, with slopes, hills, or rocky outcroppings, or if there are mature trees or specimen plants that will remain, it may be difficult to carry out a formal design. Such a site lends itself naturally to an informal plan, and most gardeners with these conditions take that course. Yards that are level and have no outstanding natural features are readily adapted to either the formal or informal style. Informal gardens have a predominance of curved, flowing lines and a seeming disregard for symmetry. The curves of lawn areas, patios, walkways, beds, and borders are usually gentle, wide arcs that follow the natural contours of the terrain. One curve leads to another, creating a feeling of natural harmony.

Formal gardens are composed primarily of straight lines and classical symmetry; that is, what appears on the right side of the garden is matched, sometimes nearly perfectly, on the left. Formal gardens are frequently rectangular,

This formal wall is softened by a handsome border of lavender, iris, columbine, and other perennials.

and this shape is repeated in other parts of the plan, in pools, patios, flower beds, and borders. A single object such as a statue, pool, or sundial often serves as the point of interest. It may be placed in the center or toward the rear of the garden, directly in the line of sight from a favorite viewing spot. A formal design is easiest to lay out and, because of its visual simplicity, is often the best choice for a small lot.

Once you have made the choice of a formal or informal style, the next step is to decide whether to plant beds or borders (or both, if there is sufficient space).

Beds and Borders

Two key elements in garden design for as long as there have been gardens are beds and borders. What are they exactly, and how do they differ? The term *bed* means a cultivated area surrounded by an open expanse, usually a grass lawn. A *border* is a cultivated area that bounds or borders an expanse, such as the perimeter of a lawn. It often adjoins a walkway. Beds and borders may be designed along either informal or formal lines.

Beds For most of today's gardeners, a formal bed seems more appropriate in a public park or on municipal grounds than in one's own backyard. Beds are generally less popular and practical than borders for the simple reason that they look best with fairly large open areas. Putting a bed into an average-sized yard is like placing a very big table in the middle of an average-sized room: It substantially reduces the free space.

Still, beds have a number of important advantages. One strong proponent of informal beds, or island beds, as he calls them, is Alan Bloom, one of the world's foremost authorities on perennials. Bloom favors beds for three reasons: first, they are accessible from all sides and hence are easier to maintain than standard borders; second, they admit more sunlight and allow better air circulation, which benefits plants; and third, they can be viewed from all sides and so offer more possibilities for the attractive arrangement of plants. If these features appeal to you, and you have the space, beds may be ideal for your garden.

Borders   The greatest advantage of borders over beds is that borders allow more open space. In a yard of standard urban or suburban dimensions, leaving the center open creates a more spacious feeling, provides space for recreation, and provides a "quiet" space to contrast with whatever visual activity there is on the perimeter of the yard—trees, shrubs, or the flower border itself.

Much of the effectiveness of a border depends upon the open space it defines. There should be a pleasing relationship between the

depth of the border (the distance from front to back) and the width of the yard. For example, if borders are proposed for both sides of a yard that is 40 feet wide, making the borders 12 feet deep would create a tunnel effect. For a more pleasing proportion between a border and the space it encloses, its total depth should never exceed more than a fourth of the total width of the yard. In the example just used, each of the borders should be 5 feet wide, leaving 30 feet open between them. (Here's the math: one fourth of 40 is 10. Since two borders are needed, 10 divided by 2 equals 5; hence, each border should be 5 feet wide.)

In addition to allowing more open space, borders serve to soften the lines of buildings, fences, walkways, and lawns.

Borders are often installed so that they are flush against a building or fence, which makes them accessible from only one side. This situation limits the border depth to about 5 feet. Having the border any deeper would make it difficult to tend plants in the back without walking on those in front. It is possible, however, to have a deeper border if a path at least 30 inches wide is left behind it on which the gardener can walk to weed, stake, groom, or prune from behind the scenes. The tall plants in the border hide this rear path from view. Having such a path also allows more of the air circulation plants need and makes the border less vulnerable to invasion by the roots of shrubs or trees behind the border.

Other design considerations are edging and, for a border, background.

Backgrounds   For backgrounds, most of us must settle for whatever currently separates our property from adjacent properties. This most often is a fence or wall but may also be a hedge, shrubs, or, in part, buildings.

The most attractive backdrop for a secluded garden is a stone or brick wall. Next best is a weathered, natural wood fence. If fences are painted or stained, they may need to be redone every few years. It's best to choose paint or stain closest to the color of the wood in its weathered state. Medium to dark browns or grays generally make the best backgrounds for flowers.

If the fence or adjacent building is unsuitable as an attractive backdrop, create a background by planting vines. Wisteria, trumpet vine,

Stone walls make an outstanding background for borders. Phlox, campanula, and cosmos combine well in this informal border of annuals and perennials.

lace vine, honeysuckle, climbing hydrangea, and ivy are just a few possible choices. The green leaves will much improve the appearance of the background, and some vines contribute their flowers to the total effect as well.

Shrubs make a particularly attractive background. If there is room, plant some, perhaps mixing evergreen and deciduous shrubs. Or plant a hedge to both block an unattractive view and provide a good dark background for the border. Needled evergreen hedges such as yew generally grow much more slowly than broadleaf hedge plants such as privet. They take fewer nutrients from the soil and are thus much slower to invade the border. If planted as gallon-sized plants, however, they may take 10 years or more to fill in completely. It may be well worth the savings in time to start with larger plants. Tall perennials can also serve as a background for the shorter flowers in the border; hollyhocks and delphiniums have long been used for this purpose. A list of large perennials suitable for backgrounds appears on page 27.

Edgings   An edging sets off a bed or border from whatever is immediately adjacent, for example, a gravel path or lawn. Edgings are useful for discouraging grass or weeds from sneaking uninvited into the border as well as for keeping gravel on the path where it belongs. They also give the border a clean, neat line.

If the bed or border fronts onto a lawn, a row of bricks laid side by side and set slightly lower than the level of the turf not only defines the planting area but makes an excellent mowing strip. Wood 2 by 4s or other milled lumber, including railroad ties, make a good straight edging. The grass does have to be trimmed by hand where it meets the wood.

For a less formal look, fieldstone set in mortar is attractive, especially if plants such as basket-of-gold or yellow-archangel are allowed to drape and trail over them. Large stones also make an excellent edging. Another easy way to define the edge of a planting area is to install the small flexible wire fencing commonly available at garden centers.

Where a walkway or lawn flanks the bed or border, many people choose to have the first row of plants grow into the lawn or pathway in a natural manner. A list of low perennials for edging the border appears on page 27.

Whatever you choose as your edging, remember that unless there is some kind of underground barrier between flowers and the lawn, there will be some extra weeding. Garden centers usually carry inexpensive rolls of metal or plastic strips for just this purpose.

Choosing Plants

Once you have made the basic decisions concerning your garden's location and style, it's time for the part of planning a perennial garden that most people find the most fun: choosing the plants. To make your choices, it's helpful to consider the following questions.

What favorite perennials fall into the "must have" category? What colors should you avoid because they would clash with an existing background wall, fence, or planting? White flowers may fade into insignificance against a white wall, and pink peonies against a barn-red fence may have the unfortunate effect of setting the teeth on edge.

Do you want a single color scheme blooming all at once or a series of color effects, with one wave of flowers giving way to the next?

Do you want a variety of shapes, sizes, and textures, or do you want plants that are more or less similar in appearance?

Are the choices restricted to small plants by limited space, or can you accommodate some of the bigger, bolder ones?

In designing a perennial garden, you need to consider several specific characteristics of perennials in order to make the best choices. Obviously, the cultural requirements of the plants must match the soil, light, and climatic conditions in your garden. In addition, it is wise to note each plant's color, height, spread, form, texture, and bloom season. Each of these characteristics plays an important role in the ultimate effect of the garden design.

Color   Perennials come in such a vast range of colors that making a choice can be confusing to the point of being overwhelming. Fortunately, some simple principles of color can help you enormously in selecting flowers and combining their colors in the garden. You'll find a list of perennials arranged by flower color on pages 28 to 30.

The color wheel on page 14 shows the basic relationships of colors to one another. Red, red-orange, orange, yellow-orange, and yellow are

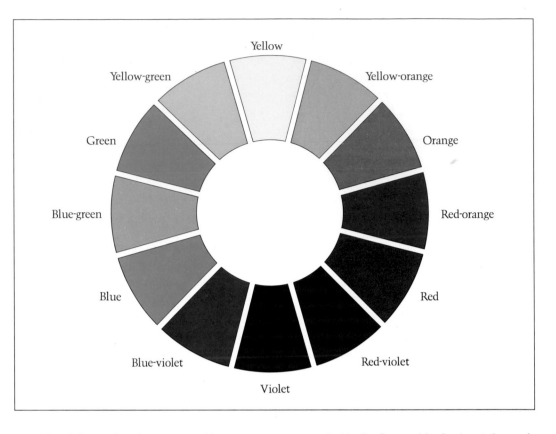

A color wheel is a diagrammatic way of showing relationships among colors. Colors on the right side of the wheel are warm. Colors on the left side are cool. Colors adjacent to each other are analogous. Opposite colors are complementary.

considered "warm" colors; green, blue-green, blue, blue-violet, and violet are considered "cool" colors. Although colors are neither warm nor cool in a physical sense, they can impart feelings of warmth or coolness, of passion or tranquillity.

To the eye, warm colors tend to advance and cool colors tend to recede. When viewed at a distance, warm colors appear closer, and cool colors seem farther away. A planting of predominantly cool-colored flowers—tall spires of dark blue delphiniums, for example—at the rear of your garden makes the yard seem larger. Warm colors, such as a bed of brilliant red and yellow red-hot-poker (*Kniphofia uvaria*), make it feel smaller. Spot plantings can have similar effects, seeming either to deepen a part of the yard or to bring it closer.

Generally, cool colors are best for close-up viewing and warm colors are better for dramatic displays. Plantings of blue bellflower (*Campanula*), violet meadow sage, and purple phlox may have substantial impact next to a patio or along a path, but planted in the distance they might be all but lost. To emphasize cool colors, plant them close to the point from which they'll most often be seen. Warm-color plants such as red daylilies (*Hemerocallis*), yellow oxeye (*Heliopsis helianthoides*), and

orange butterfly flower (*Asclepias tuberosa*), can bring a distant part of the yard into sharp focus. When combining warm and cool colors, keep in mind that warm colors can easily overwhelm the cooler colors.

A *hue* is a pure color. A *tint* is lighter than the pure color and a *shade* is darker. In combining hues, tints, and shades, there are four classic schemes.

Monochromatic color schemes are those with flowers in various tints and shades of one color. No garden is truly monochromatic, of course, because the green of the leaves is always present. Some of the world's most beautiful gardens have used monochromatic schemes.

Analogous color schemes use colors closely related to one another on the color wheel. Any three adjoining colors are said to be analogous; for example, yellow-orange, yellow, and yellow-green. Gertrude Jekyll used yellow-orange black-eyed-susans (*Rudbeckia fulgida* var. *sullivantii* 'Goldsturm'), yellow-green thinleaf sunflowers (*Helianthus decapetalus* var. *multiflorus*), and clear yellow mullein (*Verbascum*), along with other yellow flowers to create an analogous scheme in her own border at Munstead Wood.

Complementary schemes combine colors opposite one another on the wheel; for example, red and green, yellow and violet, and orange and blue. These are powerful combinations, jarring to some, vibrant to others. They are best with pure colors, rather than shades or tints, for example, scarlet Oriental poppies (*Papaver orientale*) growing up through dark green bird's-foot ivy or yellow false-lupine (*Thermopsis caroliniana*) with blue-violet speedwell (*Veronica longifolia* 'Blue Peter'). To blend strong complementary colors, arrange them to intermingle where the edges meet rather than keeping them in clearly defined clumps. Silver-leaved or white-flowered plants such as wormwood (*Artemisia schmidtiana*) or baby's breath (*Gypsophila paniculata*) soften the impact of bold combinations. Leading up to the brightest colors with flowers of similar color but somewhat less intensity also tones down the impact a bit, for example, combining hot-pink asters with paler pink chrysanthemums.

Polychromatic schemes produce a carnival-like atmosphere in the garden. They may combine any colors and every color. These are often the result of random plantings. There is nothing wrong with this, and, in fact, it can lead to some happy surprises—accidental but especially pleasing color combinations that become the mainstay of the garden for seasons to come.

Foliage color is also a consideration. Perennials have foliage in all shades and tints of green, in blue-green, blue-gray, silvery blue, silvery gray, and gray. Leaves may also be variegated. It's generally a good idea to avoid plants with variegated foliage. They are notoriously difficult to combine with flowers. Plants with silver or gray foliage, however, have been the pets of many gardeners over the years. Wormwood (*Artemisia*), lamb's-ears (*Stachys*), and mullein (*Verbascum*) are a few of the silver or gray-foliage plants that are striking combined with flowers. They are especially effective with white or pale blue to lavender flowers.

Height   Perennials range in height from less than a foot to as tall as 12 feet. The standard rule for borders is to stair-step the plantings, with the shortest plants in front, medium-height plants in the middle, and the tallest ones in the back. In island beds of mixed plantings, the tallest flowers need to be toward the center where they don't obscure the shorter plants. If you follow these rules strictly, however, the result is likely to be too static a combination. Bending rules a bit gives a more natural effect and a prettier garden, as long as the shorter flowers aren't completely hidden. Lists of perennials arranged by height appear on page 27.

Spread   The spread of a plant at maturity is extremely important in garden planning. Unfortunately, it is commonly overlooked by gardeners. Newly planted beds or borders, if planted with the correct spacings between plants, look painfully sparse, with more bare soil than anything else. In the eagerness for a lush, full garden, the natural temptation is to fudge a little (or a lot) and space the young plants closer together than recommended. Although it seems an awful nuisance to look up the spread of each plant and allow for it in your plan, rest assured that if you do not do so, your border or bed will turn into a jungle of scraggly, leggy, rangy plants with disappointingly few flowers. Harsh competition for light, water, and nutrients does not improve the appearance of most ornamental plants. Allowed sufficient room to grow, flowers can grow to their full size and glory.

Form   Plants have their own forms, an important design consideration. For all practical purposes, there are five basic forms in flowering plants: rounded, vertical, open, upright and spreading, and prostrate. Some gardens are composed of only one form, for example, the carefully clipped, rounded forms typical of Japanese gardens; others alternate and repeat certain forms, for example, the traditional English border with its tall vertical spires of blue chimney bellflower (*Campanula pyramidalis*) behind the rounded forms of white Paris daisy (*Chrysanthemum frutescens*) edged by low-growing pale blue Carpathian harebell (*Campanula carpatica*). Many outstanding beds and borders are made up of complementary forms, mixing the rounded with the vertical. If visualizing form doesn't come easily to you, it helps to imagine the garden in silhouette. Lists of perennials by form appear on page 28.

Although their characteristics are too subtle to play a major role in garden design, you may also want to think about flower forms. The forms that perennial blooms take are too numerous and complex to enumerate here, but some examples are the bell-shaped bellflower (*Campanula*), daisylike sunflower (*Helianthus*) or aster, spherical peony (*Paeonia*), cup-shaped marshmarigold (*Caltha palustris*), spurred columbine (*Aquilegia*), frilly or lacy pinks (*Dianthus*), star-shaped blue-star (*Amsonia*), and trumpet-shaped daylily (*Hemerocallis*). Flowers may also be borne singly at the ends of stems, in clusters, or in spikes.

The sunflower family (*Compositae*) is so large that it's all too easy to plan a garden with an overabundance of daisy-shaped flowers. The most interesting gardens, like the best bouquets, are those with a variety of different flower shapes. Midnight blue delphinium, white baby's breath (*Gypsophila paniculata*), and blue Japanese iris make a striking bouquet and an equally striking combination in the garden.

Texture   The term *texture* refers to the textural appearance of a plant, not the way it feels to the touch. The leaves may be bold, medium, or fine in texture. Texture is determined by such factors as how dense the foliage is, the shape of the plant, and how close the flowers are to one another. For example, texturally speaking, golden groundsel (*Ligularia dentata*) is bold, peonies medium, and wormwood (*Artemisia*) fine.

Like color, texture can be used to create spatial illusions in the garden. Bold-textured plants tend to seem closer, whereas plants that are fine-textured tend to recede into the distance. To make the far end of a long, narrow border appear closer, plant bold-textured plants at that end, for example, bear's-breech (*Acanthus mollis*). Fine-textured plants make a shallow border appear deeper, for example, wormwood (*Artemisia*) edging white meadowsweet (*Astilbe*) backed by white Japanese anemone (*Anemone* × *hybrida*) and white goatsbeard (*Aruncus dioicus*). The pale colors of the flowers and the fine texture of the plants both contribute to the illusion of greater depth. A list of perennials especially valuable for textural effects can be found on page 33.

Bloom season   The most important single aspect of perennial gardening is timing the bloom. When designing with perennials, it is essential to know when each plant will bloom and for how long. Different perennials bloom at different times throughout the season and for different lengths of time. The challenge is to get them to coincide. Bright yellow daffodils and dark blue dwarf delphiniums would make a lovely combination, but the daffodils bloom in early spring and the dwarf delphiniums in midsummer. It is critical to coordinate the timing to produce combinations that work. This is the most interesting, most challenging, and most exciting aspect of perennial gardening.

This coordination is crucial because perennials generally bloom for two to four weeks, a much shorter time than annuals, which typically bloom from spring through summer into early fall. (Note that there are many exceptions among perennials, and these exceptions may bloom for a much longer time. For example, chrysanthemums bloom from August to November.) To extend color over time, select plants with different blooming times or lengths of bloom. If, for instance, the goal were to have a red and yellow combination in the garden from spring to fall, the first combination might be red and yellow tulips from March through April, followed by red-hot-poker (*Kniphofia uvaria*) and yellow coreopsis from June through July, succeeded by cardinal flower (*Lobelia cardinalis*) and golden groundsel (*Ligularia dentata*) in August, and yellow chrysanthemums with showy stonecrop (*Sedum spectabile* 'Autumn Joy' or 'Meteor') from September to November.

Some gardeners select flowers that all bloom at approximately the same time for a garden filled with color. This creates a spectacular, but brief, display. Unfortunately, it also means there is little or no perennial bloom for the rest of the season. Other gardeners prefer a longer duration of color and plant for a continuous succession of bloom, with new flowers coming on as others fade past bloom. This dilutes the effect of the overall garden color. It does, however, reveal rather more of the character of the plants. In general, even when the garden is planned and planted for a succession of bloom, there are three or four peak periods during the season, interspersed with periods of green quietude.

Although it may be difficult to envision these changing patterns, a time-lapse film of a perennial border taken from early spring to late summer would clearly show one wave of flowers replacing another. See the series of photographs on page 17 showing how a perennial garden changes from season to season.

To select perennials for a succession of bloom, use the chart on pages 18 to 21, which illustrates clearly how various perennials relate to one another in terms of when they bloom and for how long.

With the variations in blossoming times and duration of bloom, the possibilities of the perennial garden are immense. Add the challenge of coordinating color to that of coordinating time of bloom and length of bloom, and the possibilities become even more immense, so great that they may intimidate the beginning gardener. You might ask, Why bother with all this? Why not merely plant annuals for a full season of bloom? The simple answer, apart from the uniquely attractive characteristics and longer life of the perennials, is that the perennial garden planned for a succession of

The four seasons of a perennial border— spring, summer, fall, and winter—are all different and all attractive. Some perennials die back to the roots, some lose their leaves, and others merely stop flowering in winter, but they all come back dependably year after year to bloom spring, summer, and fall.

Bloom Chart

	Jan	Feb	Mar	Apr	May	Jun	Jul	Aug	Sep	Oct	Nov	Dec
Helleborus niger	▓	▓	▓	▓								
Helleborus lividus corsicus		▓	▓									
Trillium grandiflorum			▓	▓								
Euphorbia myrsinites			▓	▓	▓							
Helleborus orientalis				▓	▓							
Aurinia saxatilis				▓	▓							
Bergenia cordifolia				▓	▓							
Brunnera macrophylla				▓	▓							
Dicentra formosa				▓	▓	▓						
Mertensia virginica				▓	▓							
Lamiastrum galeobdolon				▓	▓							
Oenothera berlandieri				▓	▓							
Oenothera missouriensis				▓	▓							
Oenothera speciosa				▓	▓							
Phlox subulata				▓	▓							
Primula vulgaris				▓	▓							
Primula × *polyantha*				▓	▓							
Primula sieboldii				▓	▓							
Pulmonaria saccharata				▓	▓							
Pulmonaria angustifolia				▓	▓							
Euphorbia epithymoides				▓	▓	▓						
Iris, bearded					▓	▓						
Aquilegia					▓	▓						
Armeria maritima					▓	▓						
Caltha palustris					▓	▓						
Dianthus plumarius					▓	▓						
Doronicum cordatum					▓	▓						
Euphorbia cyparissias					▓	▓						
Geranium sanguineum					▓	▓	▓					
Geum hybrids					▓	▓	▓					
Iris, Pacific Coast					▓	▓						
Iris pseudacorus					▓	▓						
Paeonia hybrids					▓	▓						
Polygonatum commutatum					▓	▓						
Primula japonica					▓	▓						
Stachys grandiflora					▓	▓						
Trollius europaeus					▓	▓						
Acanthus mollis					▓	▓						

Bloom Chart

	Jan	Feb	Mar	Apr	May	Jun	Jul	Aug	Sep	Oct	Nov	Dec
Amsonia tabernaemontana					▓	▓						
Baptisia australis					▓	▓						
Dicentra eximia					▓	▓	▓	▓				
Dicentra spectabilis					▓	▓						
Dictamnus albus					▓	▓						
Hemerocallis hybrids						▓	▓	▓				
Thalictrum aquilegifolium					▓	▓	▓					
Alchemilla mollis						▓	▓					
Anchusa azurea						▓	▓					
Asclepias tuberosa						▓	▓	▓				
Astilbe						▓	▓					
Calamagrostis epigeous (a grass)						▓	▓	▓				
Campanula glomerata						▓	▓					
Campanula carpatica						▓	▓	▓				
Campanula lactiflora						▓	▓	▓	▓			
Chrysanthemum coccineum						▓	▓					
Chrysanthemum × superbum						▓	▓	▓				
Coreopsis lanceolata						▓	▓					
Coreopsis verticillata						▓	▓	▓				
Delphinium elatum						▓		▓	▓			
Dianthus × allwoodii						▓	▓	▓				
Dianthus caryophyllus						▓	▓					
Dianthus deltoides						▓	▓					
Digitalis purpurea						▓	▓					
Filipendula vulgaris						▓	▓					
Gaillardia × grandiflora						▓	▓	▓	▓			
Arrhenatherum elatius (a grass)						▓	▓					
Heuchera sanguinea						▓	▓					
Kniphofia uvaria						▓	▓	▓	▓			
Lupinus Russell hybrids						▓	▓					
Lychnis chalcedonica						▓	▓					
Lychnis coronaria						▓	▓					
Lychnis × haageana						▓	▓					
Lysimachia nummularia						▓	▓	▓				
Lysimachia punctata						▓		▓				
Oenothera berlandieri						▓	▓					
Papaver orientale						▓						
Penstemon hartwegii						▓	▓					

Bloom Chart

	Jan	Feb	Mar	Apr	May	Jun	Jul	Aug	Sep	Oct	Nov	Dec
Salvia pratensis						▓						
Salvia × superba						▓						
Scabiosa caucasica						▓	▓	▓				
Thermopsis caroliniana						▓						
Tradescantia virginiana						▓	▓					
Veronica incana						▓	▓					
Veronica latifolia						▓	▓					
Iris sibirica						▓						
Achillea						▓	▓	▓				
Aruncus dioicus						▓	▓					
Chrysogonum virginianum						▓	▓	▓	▓			
Cimicifuga racemosa							▓	▓				
Coreopsis grandiflora						▓	▓					
Filipendula rubra						▓	▓					
Filipendula ulmaria						▓	▓					
Deschampsia caespitosa (a grass)						▓	▓					
Iris kaempferi						▓	▓					
Monarda didyma						▓	▓					
Veronica hybrids						▓	▓					
Crambe cordifolia					▓	▓						
Anthemis tinctoria						▓	▓	▓				
Campanula persicifolia						▓	▓					
Campanula pyramidalis							▓	▓				
Campanula rapunculoides						▓	▓	▓				
Catananche caerulea						▓	▓					
Agapanthus orientalis							▓	▓				
Chrysanthemum parthenium							▓	▓				
Echinacea purpurea							▓	▓				
Echinops exaltatus							▓	▓				
Euphorbia corollata						▓	▓					
Gypsophila						▓	▓					
Heliopsis helianthoides scabra							▓	▓	▓			
Hosta sieboldiana							▓					
Hosta undulata							▓					
Hosta ventricosa							▓	▓				
Liatris							▓	▓				
Lysimachia clethroides							▓	▓				
Lythrum salicaria							▓	▓				

Bloom Chart

	Jan	Feb	Mar	Apr	May	Jun	Jul	Aug	Sep	Oct	Nov	Dec
Platycodon grandiflorus							■	■	■			
Schizachyrium scoparium (a grass)							■	■	■	■	■	■
Stachys officinalis							■	■				
Stokesia laevis							■	■				
Thalictrum rochebrunianum							■	■				
Verbascum olympicum							■	■				
Veronica longifolia							■	■				
Veronica spicata							■	■				
Belamcanda chinensis							■	■				
Boltonia asteroides							■	■	■	■		
Helenium autumnale							■	■				
Hibiscus moscheutos							■	■				
Lobelia cardinalis							■	■				
Phlox paniculata							■	■	■			
Rudbeckia							■	■				
Salvia azurea							■	■				
Stachys byzantina							■	■				
Aster								■	■	■		
Belamcanda flabellata								■				
Ceratostigma plumbaginoides								■	■			
Chrysanthemum hybrids								■	■	■	■	
Cimicifuga americana								■	■			
Cimicifuga dahurica								■	■			
Cortaderia selloana (a grass)								■	■			
Molinia caerulea (a grass)							■	■				
Helianthus decapetalus								■				
Hosta fortunei								■				
Hosta decorata								■				
Hosta lancifolia								■				
Ligularia dentata								■				
Pennisetum alopecuroides (a grass)								■	■			
Sedum spectabile								■	■			
Solidago hybrids								■	■			
Anemone × *hybrida*								■	■	■		
Miscanthus sinensis (a grass)								■	■	■	■	■
Hosta plantaginea								■	■			
Cimicifuga foetida								■	■			
Hosta tardiflora									■	■		

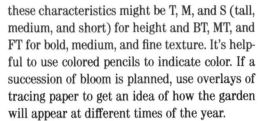

bloom is always changing. The perennial garden is not one garden for one year, but many gardens in one for many years.

The "Plant Selection Guide" that begins on page 49 is an ideal way to find out a great deal about many different perennials quickly and easily. For each plant, it lists all of the previously mentioned characteristics: cultural requirements, color, height, spread, form, texture, and bloom season. The lists beginning on page 27 make the task of choosing plants for different characteristics and cultural conditions fairly uncomplicated. Additional sources for plants and plant information are given on page 108. It's a good idea to make a list of plants that sound as though they would work well in your garden, so that you have it handy when the time comes to lay out the garden plan on paper.

Mapping the Garden

Once you have reviewed the design basics and decided upon some plants, it's time to draw up a garden plan. Graph paper makes it fairly simple to get a realistic picture of your space and proportions. It's easiest to work with paper that has 4 squares to the inch, allowing each square to represent 1 square foot of garden space.

Outline the shapes of your beds and borders on the paper. Number the list of plant choices, and write the numbers on the plan in the position you are considering for each plant. Include information on various plant characteristics to get a better picture of the garden. Symbols for

Mixed borders combining annuals and perennials provide more bloom for a longer period than perennials alone and involve less work replanting every year than annuals alone.

these characteristics might be T, M, and S (tall, medium, and short) for height and BT, MT, and FT for bold, medium, and fine texture. It's helpful to use colored pencils to indicate color. If a succession of bloom is planned, use overlays of tracing paper to get an idea of how the garden will appear at different times of the year.

The plan can be simple or complex. Draw as many plans as it takes to find a garden plan that clicks.

Planning a Mixed Border

There is no law that says a perennial border must be limited to perennials. In fact, if a fairly steady blaze of color is the goal, you will need more than just perennials. Even Gertrude Jekyll was not above sinking pots of color grown on elsewhere into the bare places left by perennials past bloom. Annuals also work well to fill in blank spaces and add extra color.

Perennials have the advantage of being permanent additions to the border and of providing a basic framework, but the warm-season annuals undeniably have a longer season of bloom. This fact makes them indispensable for color early in the season before the perennials come into bloom or to succeed those that are past bloom.

Many of the most beautiful flower beds and borders in the world have predominantly perennial plants, but annuals, bulbs, flowering shrubs, and other plants are integral to the total effect. Limiting the choices to perennials exclusively means missing out on such charming combinations as yellow nasturtiums and blue salvia or deep purple heliotrope and dark rose beardtongue (*Penstemon*). Gertrude Jekyll, in her garden at Munstead Wood, combined scarlet dahlias with Oriental poppies (*Papaver orientale*), and wakerobin (*Trillium grandiflorum*) with Solomon's-seal (*Polygonatum*) and lily-of-the-valley (*Convallaria majalis*).

Spring- and summer-flowering bulbs are also important to any flower border, if only for the variety of unusual flower shapes they provide: tulips, hyacinths, cyclamen, scilla, camas, and daffodils of all shapes and sizes are but a few of the spring-blooming bulbs that bring life and color to the border well in advance of most perennial and annual bloom. The midsummer border can be made more interesting by adding tall summer lilies, *Amaryllis belladonna*, and the dozens of varieties of dahlia and allium.

The greatest drawback to an all-perennial border is that it is bare in winter. Planting a few hardy shrubs or small trees will give you something to look at during the long, dark months of winter, to bear witness that there is indeed a garden under all that snow or sodden soil. Choose shrubs or small trees that won't outgrow their allotted space, and look for varieties with some interesting fall or winter characteristics, such as bright foliage, berries, or an attractive branch pattern when the plant is bare. Such trees include dwarf forms of crab apple or flowering cherry, Japanese maple, dogwood, or flowering chestnut. The Japanese maple 'Sangokaku' has bright red branches that make a dramatic silhouette against snow and gleam brilliantly when rinsed with rain. Several dogwoods also have colored twigs and branches: Tatartian dogwood (*Cornus alba*), Siberian dogwood (*C. alba* 'Sibirica'), and bloodtwig dogwood (*C. sanguinea*) all have red branches for winter color as well as attractive flowers in May and June. Yellowtwig dogwood (*C. sanguinea* 'Flaviramea') has yellow twigs and branches. Trim dogwoods back hard after they bloom to get the new growth that gives the best winter color. Rose-gold pussy willow (*Salix gracilistyla*) adds early spring interest; you can keep it to size by cutting the branches for arrangements or by pruning it to 2 feet every three or four years. Dwarf hollies, dwarf junipers, and hebe can be incorporated into beds and borders for year-round interest.

Restoring a Garden

More and more people are buying older homes with the intention of restoring them to their original architectural style. Victorian houses, Arts-and-Crafts-style bungalows, shingle-style cottages, colonial farmhouses, and brownstone row houses frequently receive massive investments of time, effort, and energy from new owners. Once the architectural restoration is done, however, the gardens often need the same care that went into the house, in order to complete the picture. Just as houses reflect their period in time, so can the gardens that surround them.

Restoring a garden to fit a period house can be frustrating because locating information on what the garden looked like in the past or what types of plants might have been grown there is seldom easy. Some good places to start looking are local libraries, historical societies, and title companies, which often maintain large collections of old photographs of the area. Although there may not be a picture of that particular house way back when, it's possible to get a feel for what the gardens of the period were like by carefully scrutinizing old photographs. Don't overlook the opportunity to talk with elderly neighbors; they may have vivid recollections of what the surrounding gardens once looked like.

Old garden books of the era will give a good idea of what plants were available and fashionable. Plant societies such as the American Rhododendron Society, the American Rose Society, and other specialist garden groups can help determine when specific species or hybrids were introduced into trade. For example, the restorer of the gardens of a 1904 shingle-style summer cottage in California chose the sweetheart rose Cécile Brünner to clamber over a rose arch because Cécile Brünner was introduced in 1881 and would have been available for the original garden. Bellflowers (*Campanula*) were added because they, too, would have been available: *C. lactiflora*, *C. glomerata*, and *C. persicifolia* were all in European gardens in medieval times. They probably arrived with the colonists and had almost certainly made their way to California by 1904. A huge clump of Gladwin iris (*Iris foetidissima*) that was already established in the garden was retained because it, too, was found in English gardens more than two hundred years ago, and so would certainly have been around in 1904. By determining what plants were available when the house was built, it's possible to plan a lovely and highly authentic period garden.

Even if the garden appears to be an overgrown jungle or a hopeless muddle, it is worth waiting a full year before going overboard with the pruning shears and before digging up plants without knowing exactly what they are. Old and irreplaceable plants may lurk there, unrecognized or hidden from view. Spring may reveal daffodils or lilies in vast numbers or in varieties no longer listed in the catalogs. The apparently dead stem that winds up over an arbor could well be an antique rose. That leafless tree might turn out to be one of the heritage apple trees now lost to gardeners by the hybridization of more-commercial varieties. Nor do dormant perennials reveal themselves until the soil warms up.

Few books deal exclusively with the restoration of period gardens, but plenty have been written on specific architectural styles. These may have chapters relevant to gardens and appropriate landscape styles. Even if no landscape information is given, photographs in books of period architecture can often suggest ideas for creating a garden that is in keeping with the period and architectural style of the house.

Planning a Cutting Garden

It's a classic gardener's dilemma: The flowers look so attractive in the garden that there is an overwhelming temptation to cut some for the house, but if the flowers are cut for the house, the garden doesn't look as nice any more. The sensible solution is to set aside some space for a cutting garden.

The cutting garden solves another pressing problem of gardening: Some flowers make splendid cut flowers but, for one reason or another, are less than lovely in the garden. Old-fashioned clove-scented carnations are a perfect example. They have a deplorable tendency to flop, and will stand up straight only if every stem is propped or staked or tied—not a particularly charming look. On the other hand, their flowers and fragrance are delightful. They are best grown discreetly out of sight in the cutting garden. Chrysanthemums are very much the same: They need regular pinching and staking to bloom well, but that much tromping about in the border doesn't exactly benefit the other flowers. Freesias, too, are inclined to collapse just as the blooms open, but how could one have spring without that wonderful fragrance? Shasta daisies are inclined to sprawl, but their big, shaggy heads are terrific in bouquets. Sweet peas have to be grown on strings or on a fence, which is utilitarian and, alas, looks it, but the flowers are so charming and smell so sweet, it's a shame to be without them. Tall delphiniums and dahlias, summer lilies, and foxglove are all excellent cut flowers, but taking enough for a good bouquet spoils the border. For these reasons, a cutting garden is preeminently useful.

Perennial flowers are among the most prized of all cut flowers, lending themselves particularly well to large bouquets of striking impact. A dozen or so red-hot-pokers in a tall glass cylinder, an armload of cobalt blue delphiniums in a big Delft blue-and-white pitcher, a combination of sunflowers and coreopsis in a rich green Provençal vase, or masses of pale pink peonies in a stone crock are just a few possibilities.

Because the cutting garden is basically utilitarian, lay it out in the simplest, most practical manner. Plant the perennials in rows like a vegetable garden, with the tallest flowers set so that they don't shade the shorter ones. A little-used side yard is an ideal place for a cutting garden as long as it receives at least a half day of sun; an isolated corner of the backyard also works well, or the little strip of land often found behind the garage. Prepare the soil properly; few things thrive in genuinely poor soil. Turn the soil at least 6 inches down, rake it free of clods or rocks, and dig in some compost before seeding or setting out seedlings.

Cut flowers keep longer if you follow a few simple rules. Cut them in the morning or evening when they are most turgid with water; flowers cut in the middle of the day are somewhat wilted, and once cut, have difficulty absorbing enough water to either look good or last long.

Use a sharp knife or pair of scissors to cut flowers, and make a clean cut. Take a pail or pitcher of warm water into the garden and plunge the stems into it immediately.

When arranging the flowers, remove any foliage from the base of the stems; leaves left underwater discolor the water and begin to smell nasty in a remarkably short time. Professional flower arrangers often cut the stems again before putting the flowers into the vase. For the longest life, cut the stems underwater and make the cut at an angle.

Cut flowers do best in a cool room out of direct sunlight. Changing the water daily also helps the bouquet last longer. Cut flower "foods" available at some garden centers and from florists can be added to the water to prolong the bloom even longer.

A cutting garden is also an excellent place to hold perennials in reserve until you are ready to plant them in the landscape or garden. For example, nurseries often put perennials on sale once they are past bloom. You can get good buys during these sales, but it's not really the best time to put the plants in the bed or border. Tuck them in the cutting garden until fall or spring. The cutting garden is also a good place to practice with a new perennial to get a feel for how well it performs in your garden before setting it out in a bed or border. If you aren't quite sure what a daylily (*Hemerocallis*) will look like in your garden, give it a year in the cutting garden to find out.

Perennials that make outstanding cut flowers appear in a list on page 32.

Planting Perennials in Containers

Perennials often make excellent container plants, especially when they are combined with annuals or bulbs. Such plantings provide a much longer season of color and a good contrast between foliage and flowers. As the early bulbs and perennials pass their prime, the annuals can fill in and cover with a summer-long display of flowers.

Some combinations with annuals, perennials, and bulbs that you might want to try are dark pink beardtongue (*Penstemon*) and a lighter pink 'Cascade' petunia; perennial blue salvia with blue trailing lobelia; 'King Alfred' daffodils with curled parsley; and the bushy 'Connecticut Yankee' delphiniums, blue hyacinths, white sweet alyssum, and 'Blue Mariner' petunias.

Container culture Containers offer the advantages of mobility and variety. They can be planted and grown on until they are ready to go on display, or they can be planted with plants already in bloom for instant color. They can be grouped on a patio or deck or around an entryway, anywhere they will add a bright note to the garden or the house. Containers also serve well to hold flowers you may wish to plant later in the garden. A good example of this is a gift of potted daffodils, paper-white narcissus, tulips, cyclamen, azaleas, or chrysanthemums. All of these plants will grow perfectly well in the garden once their blooms have faded in the house.

Garden centers, nurseries, and variety stores offer wide selections of containers in all sizes made of terra-cotta (clay), ceramic, plastic, and wood. They also have rectangular planters, square boxes, and wooden half-barrels. Experienced container gardeners choose the largest containers possible; the bigger the container, the more soil it holds. That means less frequent watering for the gardener, more root room for the plants, and more space to experiment with different combinations of plants.

Soak clay pots thoroughly before planting in them. Clay is very porous, and dry pots absorb moisture from the soil of freshly potted plants, leaving less available for the flowers. Cover the drainage holes with broken pieces of pottery, irregularly shaped stones, or a small piece of fine-mesh screen. (It is not necessary to provide additional drainage with a layer of gravel or stones on the bottom.)

Fill the containers with garden soil if the soil is a good loam with excellent drainage. If your soil is marginally acceptable, mix it in equal proportions with an organic soil amendment such as peat moss, compost, or redwood soil conditioner to make it a lighter, looser growing medium more conducive to growing plants in confined quarters. Repeated waterings tend to compact soil until there is very little air space left, making drainage very slow.

If there are problems with the soil—it's too sandy or too claylike—use commercial potting soil instead. A number of prepackaged soil mixes are sold under a variety of brand names.

Before planting, water the container thoroughly, and let the soil settle. After settling, the soil should be 2 to 3 inches below the container rim. There should be enough space between the rim and the soil so that one watering will moisten the rootball completely and drain

Perennials can turn a container into a permanent living bouquet, as the statice, geraniums, and ivy do in this formal urn.

This combination of rambunctious black-eyed-susans with ornamental grasses is a low-maintenance way to use perennials. The flowers provide color, the graceful grasses provide enticing movement, and the stiff, spiky-leaved yuccas provide superb contrast with the dancing grasses.

through. If the container is too full, requiring several waterings to completely soak the roots, watering becomes a time-consuming and aggravating chore. Because of the limited amount of soil available, plants in containers need more attention than plants in the open ground. During the hot summer months, daily watering is commonly needed, especially if the containers are in a sunny or windy location. These repeated waterings leach nutrients out of the soil rather quickly. To compensate for this loss, most successful container gardeners apply liquid balanced fertilizers at half-strength every two weeks. Drought crystals, available at most nurseries, can help reduce the need for watering frequently, and save water as well.

To keep flowers looking their best, pinch off any dead flowers or leaves regularly.

A FRESH TWIST ON PERENNIAL GARDENING

It is often said that there is nothing really new in gardening, and it is certainly true that most new trends in gardening tend to be a revival of some sort, a rediscovery of a form of gardening from the past. However, the landscape architecture firm of Oehme, van Sweden & Associates in Washington, D.C., has in recent years designed a number of dramatic gardens, the likes of which have not been seen before. The plants are not new, but the way they are being used and the aesthetics behind the garden design are fresh and different enough to constitute a new form of gardening.

The concept behind these gardens is the creation of a low-maintenance landscape using masses of a limited number of different plants, the majority of which are perennials. But these gardens don't resemble the English perennial border even remotely. Rather than emphasizing flower combinations, these gardens are carefully thought-out displays of contrasting textures and forms, with a subtle use of color that changes constantly with the seasons.

A garden by Oehme, van Sweden & Associates might start out in early spring with a massive display of naturalized daffodils or grape hyacinths, bulbs that can remain undisturbed for years and that multiply in the process. These are followed in early summer by the lush new growth of black-eyed-susans (*Rudbeckia hirta*), showy stonecrop (*Sedum spectabile*), fountain grass (*Pennisetum alopecuroides*), eulalia grass (*Miscanthus sinensis* 'Gracillimus'), and plume poppies (*Macleaya* species). In midsummer the black-eyed-susans begin to bloom in what can only be described as a huge outdoor bouquet (see photograph above), followed shortly by the plume poppies. In late summer the grasses start to send up their feathery plumes, followed by the flowering stonecrop. The stonecrop flowers start out pale greenish white and, as the weather turns progressively cold, change from pink to a deep, dusky rose.

Instead of trimming off all the spent flowers and dried leaves, the plants are left in their natural state through the first hard frosts and snow. What remain are the dried leaves and seed spikes of the grasses; the dark seed heads of the black-eyed-susans; and the bronze flowers of the stonecrop. The winter garden looks like an oversized arrangement of dried flowers and leaves. These unusual gardens dramatically illustrate the extraordinary creative possibilities in designing with perennials.

PERENNIAL PERFORMERS

The following lists of perennials are categorized by plant height, form, color, application to special problems, and use. The lists are an invaluable tool for the gardener who needs to organize many different elements into a cohesive whole. Use them to spark your imagination or to solve landscaping problems. Keep in mind that, in many cases, when a name appears on a list, only selected varieties (usually too numerous to mention in the list) may fit the given category. Consult the "Plant Selection Guide," seed catalogs, and local experts to help pinpoint the variety best suited to your needs.

Large Plants

Large perennial plants provide a general effect of mass, with their dense foliage serving as backdrop to a border. An asterisk (*) indicates that the plant may reach 5 feet or more.

Aruncus dioicus	Goatsbeard
Baptisia australis	False-indigo
Boltonia asteroides	Boltonia*
Crambe cordifolia	Heartleaf crambe*
Delphinium elatum	Delphinium
Grasses:	
Cortaderia selloana	Pampas grass*
Miscanthus sinensis	Eulalia grass*
Schizachyrium scoparium	Little bluestem
Helianthus decapetalus	Sunflower
Hibiscus moscheutos	Rosemallow*
Thalictrum rochebrunianum	Lavender-mist meadowrue
Thermopsis caroliniana	False-lupine
Verbascum olympicum	Olympic mullein

Low Plants

Low perennial plants grow to no more than 18 inches in height and are useful in the front of a border, for edging, or in front of taller, leggy plants. Those marked with an asterisk (*) have the additional quality of spreading by forming mats or trailing across the ground and are useful in beds or as ground covers.

Achillea ptarmica	Yarrow
Alchemilla	Lady's-mantle*
Armeria	Sea-pink*
Artemisia	Wormwood
Aster, selected varieties	Aster
Astilbe	Meadowsweet*
Aurinia	Basket-of-gold*
Bergenia	Bergenia*
Brunnera	Siberian bugloss*
Campanula carpatica	Carpathian harebell
Ceratostigma	Blue plumbago*
Chrysanthemum	Hardy chrysanthemum hybrids, selected varieties
Chrysanthemum parthenium	Feverfew
Chrysogonum	Goldenstar*
Dianthus	Pink*
Gaillardia	Blanket-flower
Geranium	Geranium
Grasses:	
Elymus arenarius	Blue lyme grass*
Festuca ovina 'Glauca'	Dwarf blue fescue
*Hakonechloa macra**	
Gypsophila repens	Creeping baby's breath*
Heuchera	Coralbells*
Hosta	Plantain lily*
Iris, dwarf bearded	Dwarf bearded iris*
Lamiastrum galeobdolon	Yellow-archangel*
Lysimachia nummularia	Moneywort*
Oenothera	Evening primrose
Phlox subulata	Moss pink*
Primula	Primrose*
Pulmonaria	Lungwort*
Sedum	Stonecrop
Stachys byzantina	Lamb's-ears*
Trillium grandiflorum	Wakerobin
Trollius	Globeflower

Vertical Accents

The plants listed here include those having an overall vertical form, with or without spiky flowers, and those with only spiky flowers.

Acanthus	Bear's-breech
Astilbe	Meadowsweet
Baptisia	False-indigo
Cimicifuga	Bugbane
Delphinium	Delphinium
Digitalis	Foxglove
Grasses:	
Cortaderia	Pampas grass
Miscanthus	Eulalia grass
Schizachyrium scoparium	Little bluestem
Iris	Iris
Kniphofia	Red-hot-poker
Liatris	Blazing-star

Ligularia dentata	Golden groundsel
Lobelia cardinalis	Cardinal flower
Lupinus	Lupine
Penstemon	Beardtongue
Primula japonica	Japanese primrose
Salvia	Salvia
Stachys grandiflora	Big betony
Thermopsis	False-lupine
Verbascum olympicum	Olympic mullein
Veronica	Speedwell

Rounded Forms

The following plants have a smoothly rounded, bushy habit of growth and are dense, in general, with foliage from top to bottom.

Artemisia	Wormwood
Aruncus	Goatsbeard
Baptisia	False-indigo
Chrysanthemum parthenium	Feverfew
Chrysanthemum × superbum	Shasta daisy
Coreopsis verticillata	Threadleaf coreopsis
Dicentra	Bleeding-heart
Dictamnus	Gasplant
Euphorbia epithymoides	Cushion spurge
Gaillardia	Blanket-flower
Geranium	Geranium
Grasses:	
Deschampsia	Tufted hair grass
Festuca	Blue fescue
Helictotrichon	Blue oat grass
Gypsophila	Baby's breath
Helenium	Sneezeweed
Heliopsis	Oxeye
Hemerocallis	Daylily
Hosta	Plantain lily
Paeonia	Peony
Sedum spectabile	Showy stonecrop
Thermopsis	False-lupine

Open Forms

The plants in this list have an open, loose form. They are best displayed when mixed and interplanted with other perennials in a border.

Aquilegia	Columbine
Echinacea	Coneflower
Echinops	Globe thistle
Helianthus	Sunflower
Lychnis coronaria	Rose campion
Papaver	Poppy
Scabiosa	Pincushion-flower
Thalictrum	Meadowrue
Tradescantia	Spiderwort

Yellow Flowers

These plants include varieties with flowers in the color range from yellow-green and yellow to orange and bronze.

Achillea	Yarrow
Alchemilla	Lady's-mantle
Anthemis	Golden marguerite
Aquilegia	Columbine
Asclepias	Butterfly flower
Aurinia	Basket-of-gold
Caltha	Marshmarigold
Chrysanthemum	Chrysanthemum
Coreopsis	Coreopsis
Delphinium	Delphinium
Digitalis	Foxglove
Doronicum	Leopard's-bane
Euphorbia	Spurge
Gaillardia	Blanket-flower
Geum	Geum
Helenium	Sneezeweed
Helianthus	Sunflower
Heliopsis	Oxeye
Helleborus	Christmas-rose
Hemerocallis	Daylily
Iris	Iris
Kniphofia	Red-hot-poker
Lamiastrum galeobdolon	Yellow-archangel
Ligularia	Groundsel
Lupinus	Lupine
Lychnis	Campion
Lysimachia nummularia	Moneywort
Lysimachia punctata	Yellow loosestrife
Oenothera missouriensis	Ozark sundrops
Paeonia	Peony
Papaver	Poppy
Penstemon	Beardtongue
Primula	Primrose
Rudbeckia	Black-eyed-susan
Solidago	Goldenrod
Thermopsis	False-lupine
Tradescantia	Spiderwort
Trollius	Globeflower
Verbascum olympicum	Olympic mullein

White Flowers

These plants include varieties with flowers in the color range from white to cream.

Acanthus mollis	Bear's-breech
Achillea ptarmica	Yarrow
Agapanthus orientalis	Lily-of-the-Nile
Anthemis	Golden marguerite

Aquilegia	Columbine
Armeria	Sea-pink
Aruncus	Goatsbeard
Aster	Aster
Astilbe	Meadowsweet
Bergenia	Bergenia
Boltonia asteroides	Boltonia
Campanula	Bellflower
Catananche caerulea	Cupid's-dart
Chrysanthemum	Chrysanthemum
Cimicifuga	Bugbane
Crambe cordifolia	Heartleaf crambe
Delphinium	Delphinium
Dianthus	Pink
Dicentra	Bleeding-heart
Dictamnus	Gasplant
Digitalis	Foxglove
Echinacea	Coneflower
Filipendula	Queen-of-the-prairie
Geranium	Geranium
Gypsophila	Baby's-breath
Hemerocallis	Daylily
Heuchera	Coralbells
Hibiscus	Rosemallow
Hosta	Plantain lily
Iris	Iris
Kniphofia	Red-hot-poker
Liatris	Blazing-star
Lupinus	Lupine
Lysimachia clethroides	Gooseneck loosestrife
Monarda	Beebalm
Oenothera speciosa	Showy evening primrose
Paeonia	Peony
Papaver	Poppy
Penstemon	Beardtongue
Phlox	Phlox
Polygonatum	Solomon's-seal
Primula	Primrose
Stokesia	Stokes' aster
Thalictrum	Meadowrue
Tradescantia	Spiderwort
Trillium grandiflorum	Wakerobin
Veronica	Speedwell

Red Flowers

These plants include varieties with flowers in colors from red to pink and pinkish purple.

Achillea millefolium 'Fire King'	Fire King yarrow
Aquilegia	Columbine
Armeria	Sea-pink
Aster	Aster

Astilbe	Meadowsweet
Bergenia	Bergenia
Campanula	Bellflower
Chrysanthemum	Hardy crysanthemum hybrids
Chrysanthemum coccineum	Painted daisy
Delphinium	Delphinium
Dianthus	Pink
Dicentra	Bleeding-heart
Dictamnus albus purpureus	Gasplant
Digitalis	Foxglove
Filipendula	Queen-of-the-prairie
Gaillardia	Blanket-flower
Geranium	Geranium
Geum	Geum
Grasses:	
Cortaderia	Pampas grass
Pennisetum	Fountain grass
Gypsophila	Baby's breath
Helleborus	Christmas-rose
Hemerocallis	Daylily
Heuchera	Coralbells
Hibiscus	Rosemallow
Iris	Iris
Kniphofia	Red-hot-poker
Liatris	Blazing-star
Lobelia cardinalis	Cardinal flower

A single color theme, where the flowers are all the same color, can pull a collection of perennials together very effectively. This border has white anemone (Anemone sylvestris) and phlox (Phlox divaricata) in bloom bordered by lady's-mantle (Alchemilla vulgaris), iris, and geranium.

Red and yellow are a hot combination, that is, a combination of warm colors. Yellow foxtail lilies (Eremurus) and yarrow (Achillea) contrast brilliantly with red Flanders Field poppies (Papaver rhoeas) and Maltese-cross (Lychnis chalcedonica).

Lupinus	Lupine
Lychnis	Campion
Lythrum	Purple loosestrife
Monarda	Beebalm
Oenothera berlandieri	Mexican evening primrose
Paeonia	Peony
Papaver	Poppy
Penstemon	Beardtongue
Phlox	Phlox
Platycodon	Balloon-flower
Primula	Primrose
Pulmonaria	Lungwort
Scabiosa	Pincushion-flower
Sedum	Stonecrop
Thalictrum	Meadowrue
Tradescantia	Spiderwort
Veronica	Speedwell

Blue Flowers

These plants include varieties with flowers in the color range from blue and violet to lavender and bluish purple.

Agapanthus orientalis	Lily-of-the-Nile
Amsonia	Blue-star
Anchusa	Bugloss
Aster	Aster
Baptisia	False-indigo
Boltonia asteroides	Boltonia
Brunnera	Siberian bugloss
Campanula	Bellflower
Catananche caerulea	Cupid's-dart
Ceratostigma	Blue plumbago

Delphinium	Delphinium
Echinacea	Coneflower
Echinops	Globe thistle
Geranium	Geranium
Hosta	Plantain lily
Iris	Iris
Lupinus	Lupine
Mertensia	Virginia bluebells
Phlox	Phlox
Platycodon	Balloon-flower
Primula	Primrose
Pulmonaria	Lungwort
Salvia	Salvia
Scabiosa	Pincushion-flower
Stachys	Lamb's-ears
Stokesia	Stokes' aster
Tradescantia	Spiderwort
Veronica	Speedwell

Cool-Summer Lovers

These plants grow best in cool-summer areas, such as mountainous or coastal regions.

Aquilegia	Columbine
Astilbe	Meadowsweet
Delphinium	Delphinium
Dicentra	Bleeding-heart
Helleborus	Christmas-rose
Ligularia	Groundsel
Lupinus	Lupine
Penstemon	Beardtongue
Primula	Primrose
Thalictrum	Meadowrue

Plants for the South

The plants in this list will perform well as far south as USDA zone 9 (see page 108). Those marked with an asterisk (*) are well adapted to zone 10.

Acanthus	Bear's-breech*
Achillea	Yarrow
Agapanthus orientalis	Lily-of-the-Nile*
Amsonia	Blue-star
Anthemis	Golden marguerite
Armeria	Sea-pink
Artemisia	Wormwood
Aruncus	Goatsbeard
Asclepias	Butterfly flower
Baptisia	False-indigo
Bergenia	Bergenia
Brunnera	Siberian bugloss
Campanula	Bellflower

Catananche caerulea	Cupid's-dart
Ceratostigma	Blue plumbago
Chrysanthemum	Chrysanthemum*
Cimicifuga	Bugbane
Coreopsis	Coreopsis*
Dicentra	Bleeding-heart
Digitalis	Foxglove
Echinacea	Coneflower
Echinops	Globe thistle
Euphorbia	Spurge*
Filipendula	Queen-of-the-prairie
Gaillardia	Blanket-flower
Geum	Geum
Grasses: All	
Helianthus	Sunflower
Heliopsis	Oxeye
Helleborus lividus corsicus	Corsican hellebore
Hemerocallis	Daylily*
Heuchera	Coralbells
Hibiscus	Rosemallow*
Hosta	Plantain lily*
Iris	Iris
Kniphofia	Red-hot-poker*
Lamiastrum galeobdolon	Yellow-archangel
Liatris	Blazing-star*
Lychnis	Campion
Lythrum	Purple loosestrife
Mertensia	Virginia bluebells
Monarda	Beebalm
Oenothera	Evening primrose*
Penstemon	Beardtongue*
Phlox	Phlox
Platycodon	Balloon-flower
Rudbeckia	Black-eyed-susan
Salvia	Salvia
Scabiosa	Pincushion-flower
Sedum	Stonecrop*
Solidago	Goldenrod
Stachys	Lamb's-ears
Stokesia	Stokes' aster*
Tradescantia	Spiderwort
Trillium	Wakerobin*
Veronica	Speedwell
Verbascum	Mullein*

Plants That Tolerate Dry Soil

These perennials will tolerate drought and poor, dry soil better than most.

Achillea	Yarrow
Amsonia	Blue-star
Anthemis	Golden marguerite

Armeria	Sea-pink
Artemisia	Wormwood
Asclepias	Butterfly flower
Aurinia	Basket-of-gold
Baptisia	False-indigo
Belamcanda	Blackberry-lily
Catananche caerulea	Cupid's-dart
Chrysanthemum parthenium	Feverfew
Coreopsis	Coreopsis
Dianthus	Pink
Echinops	Globe thistle
Euphorbia	Spurge
Gaillardia	Blanket-flower
Geranium	Geranium
Grasses:	
Cortaderia	Pampas grass
Elymus arenarius	Blue lyme grass
Festuca	Blue fescue
Miscanthus	Eulalia grass
Schizachyrium scoparium	Little bluestem
Hemerocallis	Daylily
Iris, Pacific Coast varieties	Pacific Coast iris
Kniphofia	Red-hot-poker
Lamiastrum galeobdolon	Yellow-archangel
Liatris scariosa	Tall gayfeather
Oenothera	Evening primrose
Rudbeckia	Black-eyed-susan
Salvia	Salvia
Sedum	Stonecrop
Solidago	Goldenrod
Stachys	Lamb's-ears
Thermopsis	False-lupine
Tradescantia	Spiderwort
Verbascum	Mullein

Mrs. Bancroft's succulent collection (including aloe, agave, and yucca) in Walnut Creek, California, is a dramatic tour de force of water-conservative gardening.

Plants That Tolerate Moist Soil

The following perennials are good choices for that difficult low, soggy spot in the garden.

Aruncus	Goatsbeard
Astilbe	Meadowsweet
Boltonia asteroides	Boltonia
Caltha	Marshmarigold
Cimicifuga	Bugbane
Filipendula	Queen-of-the-prairie
Hibiscus	Rosemallow
Iris kaempferi	Japanese iris
Iris pseudacorus	Water flag iris
Lobelia cardinalis	Cardinal flower
Lysimachia	Loosestrife
Lythrum	Purple loosestrife
Mertensia	Virginia bluebells
Monarda	Beebalm
Primula japonica	Japanese primrose
Tradescantia	Spiderwort
Trillium grandiflorum	Wakerobin
Trollius	Globeflower

Plants for Shady Areas

Some of the following plants tolerate shade well, while others actually prefer it. For most shade lovers, filtered shade is ideal. Those marked with an asterisk (*) tolerate deeper shade. No plant will survive long in darkness.

Acanthus	Bear's-breech
Alchemilla	Lady's-mantle
Anemone	Anemone
Aquilegia	Columbine
Aruncus	Goatsbeard
Astilbe	Meadowsweet
Bergenia	Bergenia
Brunnera	Siberian bugloss*
Campanula	Bellflower
Ceratostigma	Blue plumbago
Chrysogonum	Goldenstar
Cimicifuga	Bugbane
Dicentra	Bleeding-heart
Digitalis	Foxglove
Doronicum	Leopard's-bane
Euphorbia	Spurge
Filipendula	Queen-of-the-prairie
Helleborus	Christmas-rose
Hemerocallis	Daylily
Heuchera	Coralbells
Hosta	Plantain lily*
Iris sibirica	Siberian iris
Ligularia	Groundsel

Lobelia cardinalis	Cardinal flower
Lysimachia	Loosestrife
Mertensia	Virginia bluebells
Monarda	Beebalm
Polygonatum	Solomon's-seal*
Primula	Primrose
Pulmonaria	Lungwort*
Thalictrum	Meadowrue
Trillium grandiflorum	Wakerobin
Trollius	Globeflower

Plants for Cut Flowers

Some of the best perennials for cut flowers are on this list. The flowers of those plants marked with an asterisk (*) are especially suitable for drying and preserving.

Agapanthus orientalis	Lily-of-the-Nile
Acanthus	Bear's-breech
Achillea	Yarrow
Anemone	Anemone
Anthemis	Golden marguerite
Aster	Aster
Boltonia asteroides	Boltonia
Catananche caerulea	Cupid's-dart
Chrysanthemum	Chrysanthemum
Coreopsis	Coreopsis
Delphinium	Delphinium*
Dianthus	Pink
Digitalis	Foxglove
Echinacea	Coneflower
Echinops	Globe thistle*
Gaillardia	Blanket-flower
Geum	Geum
Grasses: most*	
Gypsophila	Baby's breath*
Helenium	Sneezeweed
Helianthus	Sunflower
Heliopsis	Oxeye
Hemerocallis	Daylily
Heuchera	Coralbells
Hosta	Plantain lily
Iris	Iris
Kniphofia	Red-hot-poker
Liatris	Blazing-star
Lupinus	Lupine
Paeonia	Peony
Papaver	Poppy
Rudbeckia	Black-eyed-susan
Scabiosa	Pincushion-flower
Solidago	Goldenrod*
Stokesia	Stokes' aster
Veronica	Speedwell

Bearded iris, lady's-mantle (Alchemilla), *and ornamental grasses do well in moist soil along the banks of this tranquil pond.*

Plants With Attractive Foliage

The following plants are especially valuable for their foliage effect. The notation (B) signifies a bold texture, (M) a medium texture, and (F) a fine texture. The notation (G) indicates gray or silvery foliage, and (E) indicates that the plant is evergreen. Many plants that generally are evergreen may be only semievergreen if grown farther north.

Acanthus (B)	Bear's-breech
Alchemilla (M)	Lady's-mantle
Amsonia (F)	Blue-star
Armeria (F, E)	Sea-pink
Artemisia (F, G)	Wormwood
Aruncus (B)	Goatsbeard
Aurinia (G)	Basket-of-gold
Baptisia (M)	False-indigo
Bergenia (B, E)	Bergenia
Coreopsis verticillata (F)	Threadleaf coreopsis
Crambe cordifolia (B)	Heartleaf crambe
Dianthus (F)	Pink
Euphorbia (M)	Spurge
Grasses: all	
Helleborus (E)	Christmas-rose
Hemerocallis (E, selected varieties)	Daylily
Heuchera (E)	Coralbells
Hosta (B)	Plantain lily
Iris kaempferi (M)	Japanese iris
Iris sibirica (M)	Siberian iris
Kniphofia (M)	Red-hot-poker
Lamiastrum galeobdolon (G, E)	Yellow-archangel
Ligularia (B)	Groundsel
Paeonia (M)	Peony
Polygonatum (M)	Solomon's-seal
Pulmonaria (M)	Lungwort
Salvia × *superba* (G)	Perennial salvia
Sedum (M)	Stonecrop
Stachys byzantina (G)	Lamb's-ears
Thalictrum (F)	Meadowrue
Verbascum olympicum (G)	Olympic mullein

Fragrant Plants

Some of the more fragrant perennials are included in the list below. An asterisk (*) indicates that the plant foliage is fragrant when crushed or bruised.

Achillea	Yarrow*
Anthemis	Golden marguerite*
Artemisia	Wormwood*
Cimicifuga	Bugbane
Dianthus	Pink
Dictamnus	Gasplant
Filipendula	Queen-of-the-prairie
Hemerocallis, selected varieties	Daylily
Hosta plantaginea	Fragrant plantain lily
Iris, bearded	Bearded iris
Monarda	Beebalm*
Paeonia	Peony
Phlox paniculata	Summer phlox
Primula, selected varieties	Primrose
Salvia	Salvia*

From the Ground Up

Perennials, like most plants, require some simple basics for good growth: a reasonably fertile soil, good drainage, sufficient sun and water, and a modicum of tender loving care. Given a little attention to the basics in the beginning, most perennials remain healthy for years.

This chapter delineates the basic principles of good perennial gardening. It describes how to evaluate your soil and bring it into good condition, where to find plants for the perennial garden, how to start perennials from seed, and how to divide perennials. Other topics include transplanting, staking, fertilizing, watering, pest and disease control—in short, just about everything a gardener needs to know to grow healthy, flourishing perennials.

Perennials, given the little extra care they need at planting time and during the fall and winter months, reward the gardener with spectacular spring and summer displays, year after year. Some perennials, such as red valerian and foxglove, bloom twice, once in the spring and again in the fall. Some, such as heliopsis and Japanese anemones, bloom well into fall. Since most perennials are dormant during the winter, the only care they require is a bit of cleanup late in autumn and perhaps a mulch to carry them through the winter in climates where winters are extreme.

With some perennials, such as ornamental grasses, the foliage remains even through severe winters, giving color, structure, and shape to the border. Golden grasses, such as reed grass, whether glittering with raindrops or ice, are beautiful all winter. Giant grasses, such as pampas grass, are a dramatic and powerful presence in the garden every season.

Perennials like these peonies, iris, and coralbells (Heuchera) *bloom beautifully and reliably year after year.*

Delphiniums, lilies, and lady's-mantle all do best in deep, rich, moist soil.

PREPARING THE SOIL

Good soil occurs naturally in some areas of the country and requires little attention from the gardener. Such soil has plenty of organic matter, ample nutrients, and a structure that allows good air and moisture circulation and a strong foothold for roots. It's generally known as good loam.

The garden—and the gardener—with such soil is much blessed. There's nothing quite like having good, rich soil to garden in without expending any effort. But if the soil is clay or sand, improve it. Nothing is so dismaying, disappointing, and disheartening as dealing with difficult soil in which few flowers thrive.

The best time to prepare the soil for perennials is a couple of months before planting. This waiting period allows amendments added to the soil to take effect. Most perennials are planted in fall or spring, so prepare soil in the summer for fall planting or in the fall for spring planting.

The first quality to look at in your soil is its texture. The two extremes in texture are clay and sand. Clay does not allow good drainage or root penetration. Sand does not retain enough moisture and drains so quickly that nutrients leach out. If the soil has too much sand or clay, it may also have a poor structure, meaning that the crumblike particles most plants need for good growth are not present. Both clay and sand, however, have their virtues, and in the right combinations make excellent soils.

There is a simple test for texture and structure that gardeners have used for centuries. First take a shovel or cultivator and dig up the soil a bit; then take a handful of soil, squeeze it in your palm, open your hand, and see what happens. If the soil holds together for a few seconds and then crumbles apart, it's good loam. If it just sits in your hand in one big lump, it is either clay or very wet. If the weather has been fairly dry, the soil has too much clay and needs improving. If the soil doesn't stick together even briefly, it's too sandy and also needs to be amended. (This test is also a good one to determine whether the soil is dry enough to cultivate or to plant.)

Improving the Soil

Improving soils that are too claylike or sandy is a matter of adding organic matter—and plenty of it—to the top layer. Organic matter is simply matter that was once living, such as compost. Adding it is the best thing you can do for the soil. It holds water and nutrients like a sponge, increasing the soil's capacity for both; it opens and loosens the soil; and as it breaks down into humus (the dark, decayed substance that gives soil its characteristic color), it forms gluelike materials that stick soil particles together in little crumbs, forming a soft, rich medium perfect for good root growth. Soil with good structure and texture is called friable soil.

Almost all organic materials are good for the soil, and there are many available. They include the materials found at most nurseries and garden centers, such as shredded bark, chunk bark, leaf mold, peat moss, and manure as well as those that gardeners can produce by themselves or get from other sources, such as sawdust, hay, lawn and garden clippings, weeds, corncobs, and compost.

The amount of organic matter to add depends upon the condition of the soil and the depth to which it needs improving. If the garden has been growing healthy plants, or even a healthy weed crop, and if there are no drainage problems, such as rain or sprinklers leaving long-standing puddles, it may not be necessary to add much. For all practical purposes, it's impossible to add too much organic matter, and whatever amount you add will improve the soil quality. (Extremely soft, fluffy, acid soils that are mostly organic matter are one of the few exceptions.) One widely observed rule of thumb is to add organic matter equal to one third to one half of the depth of soil that needs to be improved; for example, add a 2- to 3-inch layer over soil 6 inches deep, a 4- to 6-inch layer over soil 12 inches deep, and so on.

If the organic matter is not fully decayed and does not already have added nitrogen (if it does, the label will say "nitrogen-fortified"), you will need to add some nitrogen. Two pounds of ammonium sulfate (or the equivalent) per 100 square feet of space prevents the organic matter from robbing the soil of the nitrogen that decay bacteria need to break it down further.

With very sticky clay soils, another amendment of great value is gypsum. Gypsum often helps to improve the structure of clay soils. It should be added at a rate of about 5 pounds per 100 square feet of space. If it works, drainage will be improved almost immediately. Extremely heavy clay soils are another problem entirely, and in some rare cases cannot by any means be made into good soil. If a heavy clay soil is the problem, ask at a local nursery or contact a county extension agent for more information before going to the expense of trying to improve it. It may be easier, less expensive, and less frustrating to construct raised beds and fill them with good soil.

Soil pH It's a good idea to check the pH of the garden's soil at the same time you test the condition of the soil. Many states offer free or low-cost pH tests. (For details call the local county extension agent.) Inexpensive testing kits are probably available at a local garden center, and the test is easy to perform.

The letters *pH* stand for the chemical term "potential hydrogen," which is a measure of acidity and alkalinity. The pH scale runs from 0, which is extremely acid, to 14, which is extremely alkaline. The middle of the scale, 7, is neutral. The vast majority of perennials grow best in neutral or slightly acid soils.

If the soil is extremely acid, add ground limestone to correct it. If alkalinity is a problem, correct it by adding a garden sulfur or ferrous sulfate. Both are available at nurseries and garden centers. Ask a nursery employee or county extension agent for the specific rates to apply. Describe the present pH of the soil, the type of soil, and what pH level is needed.

Fertilizer When you add organic matter and lime or sulfur to the soil, it's good to add a complete fertilizer as well. Packaged dry fertilizers are the easiest to apply. Choose a formulation such as 5-10-5 (the numbers refer to the percentages of nitrogen, phosphorus, and potassium) that is high in phosphorus and relatively low in nitrogen. Apply it at about 3 to 5 pounds per 100 square feet. A fertilizer high in nitrogen content may stimulate leaf growth at the expense of flowers, which makes for a large, lush plant with few flowers. Phosphorus stimulates both root growth and the formation of flowers. Potassium, or potash, contributes to stem strength as well as increases resistance to disease.

Cultivating the Soil

If the simple hand test mentioned earlier indicated that the soil is ready to be worked (that it is neither too claylike or sandy nor too wet or too dry), the first step is to clear the site of all weeds. It's far better to dig or pull the weeds out than to hoe or scrape them off. Pulling or digging gets the roots out; hoeing or scraping may not, and the weeds will sprout

Cutting gardens don't require elaborate design, just good soil, sun, and water to produce lots of flowers for the house. Perennial cutting gardens are easy to maintain since they don't have to be replanted each season.

again. The next step is to turn the soil over, being careful to remove any remaining weed roots: the spade or rotary tiller will chop these up if you don't get them and will, in effect, multiply the number of weeds that you must deal with later.

Once the weeds are gone, spread the organic matter, fertilizer, and, if needed, the lime or sulfur, all in a more or less even layer on top.

There is no point in being stingy at this stage; small amounts of any amendment will not change the soil structure appreciably, so spread the organic matter around with a free hand. If you are using peat moss, be sure it is moist when you take it from the bag. If not, moisten it with warm water while it is still in the bag, or use a wetting agent especially made for this purpose, which is available at garden centers. Otherwise, peat moss takes an interminable time to become incorporated into the soil.

Now the soil is ready to be dug and turned. This means using a shovel, spade, or digging fork to turn the top layer, breaking clods into smaller pieces in the process. Those with fairly large gardens are wise to use a power tiller.

To produce the best possible planting bed, cultivate by hand. Cultivating by hand makes it possible to turn the soil to a depth of 10 inches, but it is undeniably hard work in the heavy clay soils that need it most. Many knowledgeable gardeners point out that since most of the feeder roots of perennials are in the top layer of the soil, digging and turning the soil to a depth of 6 to 8 inches is quite deep enough to produce healthy, vigorous plants. In heavy soils, a digging fork is easier to use than a shovel or spade. Break up large clods and rake out all weeds and rocks.

Ideally, it's best to leave the bed fallow for a couple of months before planting. Be sure to keep weeds pulled in the meantime to keep them at a minimum in the garden.

Power tillers If you use a rotary tiller to incorporate the amendments into the soil, keep in mind that the heavier the machine, the easier the work. Power tillers are available for rent in most communities.

Make sure the soil is moist, but not wet, before beginning. If it is too dry, water the soil thoroughly, and then wait a few days to let it dry out somewhat before tilling. If the soil is unusually heavy, it may take several passes with the tiller to cultivate the soil to a depth of 6 inches.

Don't overdo it; a couple of passes should make a perfectly good planting bed and any more may make the soil so fine that the first application of water will produce a thick crust on the soil surface. Most power tillers are limited in the depth they can cultivate, usually to 6 to 8 inches. It is generally believed that the deeper the soil is cultivated for perennials, the better the results will be, especially with heavy clay soils, but there is no need to dig deeper than 10 inches.

After tilling, use a large metal rake to smooth the surface.

FINDING PLANTS

The fact that perennials have been the favorite plants of generations of gardeners is good testimony to their value in the present-day garden. The legacy of these gardeners is that today there are thousands of varieties of perennials to choose from, a selection to keep the most ambitious gardener busy and content for a lifetime.

Once you have decided how perennials are to be used in the landscape—in beds, borders, simply spotted around the garden, or as container plants—it's time to make a plant list. Compile the list from the "Plant Selection Guide" that begins on page 49 of this book, other books, garden catalogs, and from plants seen and admired in other gardens or at a local nursery or garden center.

The best sources for plants are nurseries and garden catalogs, but don't fail to consider plants given by or exchanged with gardening friends. Plants "passed over the fence" can come to be the most treasured flowers in the garden, for each year's bloom brings back memories of a friend or neighbor.

As perennials outgrow their allotted spaces, they need to be divided, and divisions from established plants are generally as good as those available from nurseries and catalogs. It's worth remembering, though, that any plant that has outgrown a neighbor's garden may well do the same in yours. The plants most frequently handed over the back fence are often the most vigorous and invasive ones. It's best to think twice about where to plant them to give them plenty of room to grow.

Nurseries

Look for a local nursery that carries a good selection of perennials. These plants will probably be well adapted to the climate of the region. Large nurseries or garden centers usually have perennials in several different stages of development, from seedling size to fully grown.

More and more nurseries are offering perennials as first-year seedlings planted in flats or plastic containers called cell packs or six-packs. These may take another year of growth in the garden to produce a good display of flowers, but the price represents a substantial savings over perennials in 4-inch pots or gallon containers.

The greatest selection of potted perennials at the nursery is always on display during their season of bloom, the spring and summer months. Obviously, it is much easier to sell plants as an impulse item when they are in full bloom, but this is also an aid to the novice gardener who doesn't mind spending the extra money to see exactly what he or she is getting.

When choosing nursery plants, select ones that are bushy and compact; avoid any that are sparse and leggy. A healthy green leaf color is a good sign that the plants have been well cared for. It's tempting to choose plants that are in full bloom, but plants without flowers are usually more satisfactory in the long run because

Rock gardens with cacti and other perennials are a good way to practice water-conservative gardening.

they have put their energy into root and leaf growth, which makes for a stronger, sturdier plant. Fresh stock is usually preferable to plants that have been growing in small containers for many months. It's a good idea to find out when the nursery receives its shipment from the wholesale grower. The gardener who is there when the truck is unloaded not only gets the freshest plants but also gets the widest selection.

Catalogs

If the selection of perennials is limited at your local nursery or garden center, order from catalogs or start perennials from seed. The list on page 108 contains many reputable sources of seeds and plants. Some of the catalogs feature perennials almost exclusively; others include other garden plants. To locate hard-to-find varieties, the specialty catalogs are best. There are, for example, thousands and thousands of irises, and few nurseries carry more than a small percentage of them. A specialty iris catalog gives a far broader range of choices.

Any charge for the catalog is usually nominal, and most companies refund its cost with your first order. Some companies print two catalogs, one for spring and one for fall. The spring catalog (the one most companies offer, and the one that most excites gardeners) is mailed in the winter; the fall catalog is usually sent out in the spring. This gives gardeners a chance to make their choices and have the plants shipped at the proper planting time.

Live perennials ordered from catalogs usually arrive in one of two ways: as dormant, bare-root plants with roots enclosed in damp sphagnum moss and wrapped in plastic, or as potted plants with the top growth visible. Companies generally are careful to note where the order is being sent and will wait to ship until the weather at the plant's destination is suitable for planting.

Catalogs serve another important function for the gardener: To sit down with a catalog filled with enticing descriptions and colorful illustrations, especially when the garden outside is wearing winter drab, is one of life's purest pleasures and a great inspiration toward the new gardening season.

Starting Plants From Seed

Starting perennials from seed is an intriguing and rewarding venture, if you have the patience, the time, and the room to try it. Planting seed has several advantages, not the least of which is that it is the least expensive way to procure a large number of plants. Another benefit is that it opens up the possibility of growing varieties other than those available at the local nursery or from mail-order catalogs. Seed selections offered by nurseries that specialize in perennials often include choice, unusual, or rare varieties that are the serious gardener's greatest temptation and challenge.

Always buy the best-quality seeds available, and plant them as soon as they arrive; the freshest seeds give the best results. Some perennials are particular about the conditions they need in order to germinate. Some need to be soaked in warm water, some need to be scarified (scratched or nicked), and very tiny (fine) seed may need to be mixed with a bit of sand before it is sown. Read the instructions included with the seeds carefully, and make every effort to provide the conditions each variety requires. The "Plant Selection Guide," which begins on page 49, includes instructions for those perennials it lists with unusual seed-starting requirements.

These freshly transplanted wax begonias and ageratum have plenty of room to grow into an attractive edging for the red-hot-poker plant (Kniphofia) *and white meadow-sweet* (Astilbe) *in this border.*

Getting started The necessary equipment includes a number of seed flats or trays with drainage holes, fresh potting soil, heating cables to provide warm soil (if necessary), and some sort of fluorescent light unit whose height above the flats can be adjusted.

Dampen potting soil in a plastic bag or other container, place it in the flats, and firm it down slightly to form a smooth, even surface. You can scatter the seeds over the surface or plant them in rows. Sow the seeds thinly, tapping them out of the packet slowly for an even spread.

The next steps depend upon the specific requirements of the seeds. Some need light and heat to germinate and others require darkness and fairly cool temperatures. Some have periods of dormancy that demand chilling. (In the interests of domestic tranquillity, do check with other members of the household before slipping flats of seeds into the refrigerator.) Some seeds, in order to germinate most quickly, need to be soaked or to have their seed coats filed. Read the instructions that come with the seeds.

Moisture is critical in seed germination. The best way to supply moisture is from the bottom, not the top. Place the flat or tray in the sink or in a larger pan, such as a cookie sheet, pour water into the sink or pan, and allow it to seep up into the soil. (Once again, it is always wise to review one's plans for the cookie sheet with other family members before spiriting it away to the potting shed or basement.) To maintain humidity, stretch a sheet of clear plastic over seeds that need light to germinate, and place a sheet of black plastic over those that need darkness. It is very important, however, to remove the plastic as soon as the seeds start to sprout; otherwise, fungus disease can wipe out the entire crop of seedlings.

Maintaining moisture is especially critical with very fine, dustlike seeds, which have a tendency to dry out quickly. It requires both time and dedication to check on seedling flats daily to be sure they are coming along.

Transplanting seedlings Once the seeds have germinated and have produced the second set of true leaves, they are ready to be planted into their own containers. Small peat pots are best, as these can be planted directly into the garden. Fill them with packaged soil mix, and wet it down thoroughly before transplanting. Be careful not to let the seedlings dry out between the time you remove them from the flat and when you tuck them safely into their new pots. This is one of the most common causes for plant loss. It's a good idea to have all the peat pots filled with soil, awaiting their new occupants, before beginning to lift the seedlings out of the flat.

Transplanting requires patience and dexterity. A flat, pointed stick such as an old plant label works well to separate the seedlings and to ease them into the new soil. Popsicle sticks sharpened to a point work nicely, too, and cuticle sticks are especially good for small, delicate seedlings. Use a light touch when firming the new soil around the roots of seedlings; too much pressure will squeeze the air from the soil, making it hard for the roots to grow.

Many perennials do not take well to transplanting. Seeds of such plants should be sown directly into peat pots. Start with 2-inch pots, and as the plants grow, plant pot and all in the next larger size of peat pot. Like clay pots, peat pots are porous and dry out quickly. Check them often to keep them evenly moist.

For the first few weeks, keep seedlings in containers in a protected environment such as an unheated sunroom, a covered porch, a lath house, or a cool greenhouse. After they are established, you can move them to a somewhat less protected environment, but they are still not ready for the full brunt of the elements. They will need more or less daily watering during warm summer months, and applications of an all-purpose complete fertilizer every four to six weeks throughout the growing season to get them on their way. Within a year's time you should have quite a collection of healthy, good-sized perennials ready to go into the garden.

Perennial seeds can be sown directly into the garden, of course, but they often have a very low rate of germination, not because the seed isn't good, but because of the rigors of natural selection: The birds eat some, the dog runs through the seed bed, the cat digs there, and the children's ball often bounces in that direction. Following the instructions just given will greatly increase germination and the degree of success with seedlings.

For more detailed information on starting seeds, see Ortho's *Color With Annuals*.

PLANTING YOUR GARDEN

Once you have prepared the soil and purchased plants or started seeds, and the weather is sufficiently warm, you are ready to set the plants out in the garden. As they grow, you will need to care for the transplants by staking, fertilizing, watering, and mulching them; dividing them when necessary; and keeping an eye out for pests and diseases.

Transplanting Dormant Plants

Dormant plants ordered from a catalog arrive sometime in early spring. They won't look like much, but they are alive and should be treated with care. If the weather does not permit planting immediately, keep them in a cool, dark spot and make sure the sphagnum moss surrounding them is kept moist.

When the time comes to plant them in the garden, remove the plants from their plastic coverings, shake the moss off carefully, and inspect the roots. Clip off any that are broken, dry, brittle, or rotted. Get them into the ground as quickly as possible; it doesn't take long for

Laying out a string grid is a simple, practical way to figure out the spacing in planning and planting a border, especially when transplanting seedlings.

wind and sun to dry out the tiny roots that are essential to life during the critical first few weeks after transplanting. Again, it's wise to have the new hole dug and puddled before taking the plant out of the plastic. (Puddling consists of watering the hole and letting it drain completely before planting the new plant.)

Before planting, take a good look at your plan to make sure you know which plants go where and how far apart they need to be spaced. Some gardeners place tiny stakes or metal plant markers to indicate locations.

Dig the holes large enough so that roots won't be cramped when they are spread out. The depth of the hole is determined by the roots of the plant. The point where the roots meet the stem or crown should be placed right at ground level.

Spread out the roots in the hole like a full skirt and pack the soil around the root system gently. When the hole is filled, firm it down by stepping on the loose soil to make sure there are no empty spaces between roots and soil. Water the plant thoroughly. This is the time to label the plants for future reference.

Transplanting Started Plants

Whether you order plants from a mail-order source or purchase them from a garden center or nursery, the planting procedure is basically the same.

To remove small plants from six-packs, push up on the bottom of the individual cell. Don't try to pull the plant out by the stem: It may not have an extensive root system and the top could break away from the roots. With a trowel, dig small holes roughly the same depth as the rootballs. Take the plants out one by one and plant them at the same level as in the pack. Firm the soil around the roots and water the plants thoroughly.

Larger perennials are often sold in plastic or metal cans. If the rootball is moist, remove the plant by turning the can over, with your hand across the top, and shaking it slightly. If the plants are in metal cans and you will be planting them right away, have the cans cut at the nursery. If the plants must wait a while to be planted, leave the cans intact and cut them later with a pair of tin snips. (Cut cans are virtually impossible to water thoroughly.) Plastic containers do not need to be cut.

Be sure to loosen any circling roots around the rootball and spread them out before planting, so that they won't girdle the plant. It's also a good idea to score the rootball with a knife; this ensures that the roots will grow out into the soil instead of growing around the rootball.

Staking

Putting in stakes is controversial among ardent perennial gardeners. Some dislike the task so much that they refuse to plant flowers that need it. Two types of plants require staking: those with tall single stalks, such as delphiniums, hollyhocks, and gladiolus; and those with floppy stems, such as asters, chrysanthemums, coreopsis, oxeyes, and carnations.

Tall, thin poles, such as the commonly available bamboo stakes, make the best supports for the single-stem plants. Simply place the stake an inch or so from the main stalk and shove it far enough into the ground to be stable. Attach the stalk to the stake with a plant tie, forming a figure eight with the tie. Be careful not to cut into the stem, and allow some room for natural back-and-forth movement.

The favored method for staking lower, bushier plants is to use metal plant stakes coated with green plastic that have an open loop at the top. They slide in easily, support the flowers inconspicuously, and can be pulled up and stored at the end of the season to be used the next year. They are fairly inexpensive, particularly considering that they can be used year after year. Most garden centers or mail-order garden-supply houses have them.

The preferred British method of staking is to take pruned branches from fruit or ornamental trees and cut them into lengths of 16 to 20 inches. When the perennials are 8 to 10 inches high, push the dried branches into the ground, placing several in a circular pattern around the perennial clump. These provide a natural framework to support the plants and will become less noticeable as they grow. This works best in areas where summer rains cause lush, luxuriant foliage to cover up the dead branches.

Fertilizing

Although not absolutely necessary, a midsummer feeding will benefit most plants. Use the same product used to condition the soil (preferably a dry fertilizer with a 5-10-5 or similar formulation), but use less: Apply about 2 pounds per 100 square feet. This ensures that the plants are well fed and go into the winter as vigorous and healthy as possible.

If any individual plants in the garden need additional feeding during the growing season, mix a liquid flower fertilizer with water and apply it to those plants only. Since it's easy to control the amount you apply, liquid fertilizers are just the thing for "touch-up" feedings. Most of the liquid formulations are fast acting. It's best to make such feedings with half-strength or even weaker solutions. Too little can be remedied; too much can't.

Liquid fertilizers are also valuable for foliar feeding, which involves spraying the fertilizer mixture onto the leaves and stems of the plant. For perennials, early spring growth is usually limited by cold soil, even when the air is warm. Under such conditions soil microorganisms are not active to convert nutrients into forms the roots can absorb. But if the nutrients were available, the plant would grow. A nutrient spray to the foliage provides immediate nourishment, allowing the plant to begin growth

Put in stakes when delphiniums are still small to avoid damaging roots or breaking flower spikes when the plants are mature. Use soft plant ties to tie the stalk to the stake.

A good way to water a freshly laid out perennial border is with a soaker hose like this one. It keeps moisture at the roots where it can encourage growth and off the leaves where it can encourage fungus diseases.

even before the roots are able to absorb food from the soil. A word of warning: If a late freeze hits, the tender new growth will be the worst damaged, and it may set the plant back severely instead of giving it a head start.

Foliar feeding is a supplement to soil nutrition, not a substitute. Nutrients applied to foliage are absorbed and used by the plant quite rapidly; absorption begins within minutes after application, and with most nutrients is completed within one to two days.

Watering

The amount of water a garden needs depends upon climate. Where summer rains are frequent, the garden may need irrigation only during an occasional dry spell. In parts of the arid West and Southwest, watering is one of the gardener's biggest chores.

Whatever the climate, the simple rule for watering correctly is this: Water well and thoroughly, and let the soil dry out between waterings. The best way to tell if the soil is watered thoroughly is to take a trowel or shovel and dig down to see if the soil is moist 3 or 4 inches deep. If it is, the water is reaching the root zone of the plants. This is absolutely essential; superficial waterings not only waste water, but they actually harm plants by encouraging the roots to grow toward the surface. Shallow roots neither feed the plant well nor anchor it securely.

Watering a flower border or bed is best done with a canvas or plastic soaker hose laid more or less permanently among the plants. Turn the water on to run steadily at a low rate to keep

the foliage as dry as possible. Try to water during the morning so that the leaves can dry off a bit before nightfall; wet foliage makes plants more susceptible to disease. Of course, it is all right to spray plants occasionally with the hose or to use overhead sprinklers to remove dust from the leaves, if it's done early enough in the morning for the plants to dry before evening.

Mulching

When spring is definitely in the air, the perennials are in the ground, the soil has warmed, and any weeds that have appeared have been pulled, apply 2 to 3 inches of mulch over the bed or border, tapering it off gradually around the plants. (A thick layer of moist mulch right next to a plant's stem can encourage pests and disease.)

Applying mulch in spring keeps the soil temperature cooler, which helps root growth. It also keeps the soil moisture at a more even level, reducing the amount of water needed, and keeps many summer weeds from becoming established. Finally, a mulch aids in the long-term development of a good soil structure. These virtues add up to better growing conditions for the plants and a much easier job of maintenance for you.

Almost any organic material can serve as mulch. The most highly recommended are finely ground fir or pine bark, pine needles, compost, well-rotted manure, and, where available, redwood soil conditioner. Peat moss, unfortunately, makes a poor mulch because it forms a crust on top that is nearly impenetrable by water.

Lots of fall leaves and access to a shredder are the infallible formula for an excellent mulch and soil amendment. Just shred the leaves, stack them in piles, and leave the piles uncovered over the winter. By spring they will have decomposed. When the weather warms, turn the pile to let it dry out enough to be applied easily. Then spread it on or dig it in with a generous hand.

In areas with extremely cold winters but not a heavy snow cover, it's important to protect plants from the threat of heaving, in which plants are forced out of the ground as a result of alternate freezing and thawing. When the soil is thoroughly frozen to a depth of 2 inches, apply a layer of open, fluffy material such as pine boughs, excelsior, salt hay, or straw over the entire bed or border. This keeps the ground frozen until spring. Note that if you apply this protection before the ground is well frozen, it may serve as a winter home for mice and other rodents still afoot, who could come to regard the roots and crowns of your plants as their winter diet.

Dividing

There are basically three reasons for dividing perennials: to control size, to rejuvenate, and to propagate.

By nature, most perennials grow larger every year, usually by spreading and making a larger clump. Left alone, the most vigorous growers can expand until they push out neighboring plants. As clumps expand, they begin to compete with themselves; the plants on the outer edge thrive in fresh soil, but those in the center suffer because they are competing for moisture, nutrients, light, and air. This can result in a circle of healthy plants around a dying center, which is not at all attractive.

Except in areas of the country with extremely cold winters (temperatures of -10° to -20° F), fall is the best time to divide perennials. The general rule is to divide spring- and summer-blooming perennials in late summer or fall and to divide fall-blooming perennials in early spring, to give them a whole growing season to reestablish themselves. In climates with extreme winters, it's best to divide in early spring rather than subject newly planted divisions to the rigors of the weather.

Before dividing, decide which plants can be saved, which to dig out altogether, and which to replant elsewhere. To make digging and dividing easier, water the bed well a few days beforehand. Prune the perennials severely, to 6 inches from the ground, so that you can see what needs to be done.

The actual dividing process is simple. Dig the entire clump out as completely as possible. If the center of the clump has died out, divide the living portion into smaller clumps to replant where you like. Where roots are so ensnarled that you can't simply pull the plants apart, cut them apart with a sharp knife. Another way to divide a stubborn clump is to insert two spading forks into it back to back, and then to press the handles toward each other, using the leverage at the tines to pry the clump apart.

Enrich the hole from which the clump was taken with some organic matter and a handful of 0-10-10 fertilizer (or some similar formulation with no nitrogen). Replace one or more of the divisions in the hole, and replant the rest elsewhere or give them away to friends who like to garden.

Controlling Pests and Diseases

As a group, perennials are remarkably free of most pest and disease problems. By taking a daily stroll through the garden, you can minimize potential problems just by keeping an eye out for anything irregular: a chewed leaf, a disfigured bud, stunted foliage, a small patch of mildew or rust on a leaf, and so on.

If you take action at the first sign of attack, less damage is likely, and the need for chemical controls is minimized.

Avoid problems by taking these steps.

• Keep old leaves picked up; they often harbor disease organisms and are safe hiding places for snails, slugs, and many damaging insects.

• Hand-pick as many pests as you can. Caterpillars, snails, and slugs all succumb nicely to stomping. A hard spray from the hose will give aphids an incentive to go elsewhere. Cutworms tossed onto the path or patio are a treat for the birds. Encourage birds in your garden with feeders and water; many birds, including hummingbirds, eat insects.

Natural mulches help keep soil temperatures a bit more even, retain moisture, and help prevent weeds from sprouting. They also keep the border looking neat and tidy.

• Pull weeds when they're small, before they can compete with surrounding plants and produce seeds. The easiest time to pull weeds is when the ground is soft from rain or watering.

• Remove and destroy any diseased leaves, flowers, or fruits. Do not put them on the compost pile; disease organisms can live from one season to the next.

• Do a thorough cleanup before winter sets in. Remove brush, dead leaves, and other likely homes for overwintering insects and diseases.

If a pest or disease is a problem in your garden, this page lists the most common problems and the best controls. Pests and diseases that affect specific plants are discussed in the "Plant Selection Guide" beginning on page 49.

Aphids   Soft-bodied, green, brown, or reddish insects that suck plant juices. *Symptoms:* Clusters of insects on shoots, flower buds, or underside of leaves. Foliage and blooms stunted or deformed. Sticky honeydew attracts ants. *Solutions:* Ladybugs feed on aphids. Wipe out aphid infestations with contact sprays such as diazinon, malathion, Sevin®, Orthene®, or insecticidal soap.

Beetles   Beetle larvae eat plant roots. *Symptoms:* Foliage, flowers, and stems are chewed, devoured, or have holes drilled in them. *Solutions:* Pick off beetles by hand or knock them into a can of kerosene and water. Spray with diazinon, malathion, or Sevin®.

Botrytis blight (gray mold)   A fungus disease that overwinters on infected plant parts. It attacks weak and dying foliage, flowers, and especially old, dying flowers. *Symptoms:* Grayish brown growth on buds and flowers often appears fuzzy. The diseased flowers come apart easily when touched. *Solutions:* Pick off and destroy faded and infected blooms. Spray with a fungicide such as chlorothalonil. Read labels for recommendations.

Caterpillars   Larvae of moths and butterflies that feed on foliage, buds, and flowers. *Symptoms:* Flower buds eaten or leaves rolled and tied around the pest and eaten from inside. Most often a problem in spring. *Solutions:* Cut out infested buds and leaves. Apply diazinon, Orthene®, or Sevin®.

Damping-off   A fungus disease that is most often a problem in damp soil. *Symptoms:* Stems of young seedlings rot at ground level and fall over. Seedlings may also fail to emerge (preemergent damping-off). *Solutions:* Do not overwater seedlings. Treat seeds with captan, benomyl, chloranil, or thiram.

Fungus diseases (include powdery mildew and rust)   Spread by wind and splashing water and overwinter on plant debris. *Symptoms:* Powdery mildew appears as white, powdery masses of spores on leaves, shoots, and buds; distorted shoots; or stunted foliage. Rust is shown by yellow dots and light green mottling on upper leaf surfaces opposite pustules of powdery, rust-colored spores on the lower surface. *Solutions:* For powdery mildew, apply benomyl or triforine. For rust, apply triforine fungicides as recommended on labels. For both, remove and destroy all infected plant parts.

Mites   Minute pests that suck juices from underside of foliage. *Symptoms:* Stippled leaves appear dry; turn brown, red, yellow, or gray; then curl and drop off. Webs may be visible on the undersides of leaves. *Solutions:* Clean up trash and weeds in early spring to destroy breeding places. Spray with Vendex® or insecticidal soaps.

Thrips   Tiny, brownish yellow, winged insects. *Symptoms:* Flecked or silver white streaking and stippling on foliage and flowers. *Solutions:* First, cut off and dispose of spent blooms. Then apply diazinon, malathion, Orthene®, or Sevin®.

Virus diseases (include mosaic and aster yellows)   Spread by propagation of infected plants, aphids, and sometimes leafhoppers. *Symptoms:* Mottling or mosaic patterns on leaves; stunted or distorted growth. *Solutions:* Dispose of entire affected plants. Prevention is the best control.

Whiteflies   Nymphs are scalelike, flat, oval, pale green, brown, or black, depending on the species. *Symptoms:* Pure white adults are easy to see. Leaves become mottled, may turn yellow and die. *Solutions:* Spray with diazinon, malathion, or Orthene®.

Starting from the upper left: aster yellows on chrysanthemums; aphids on foxglove; chrysanthemum mosaic on chrysanthemums; cucumber beetles on coreopsis; powdery mildew on delphiniums; caterpillar on a geranium.

Plant Selection Guide

Including the enormous number of cultivars and varieties, there are literally thousands of perennials from which to choose. How, then, to select the best ones for your garden?

Use this guide as you plan and design the garden or to determine the needs of perennials already in the garden. This guide lists more than one hundred perennials. With it, you can select perennials to create specific effects or to solve problems.

This guide begins the selection process. Rather than discussing all of the available perennials, it presents the species and varieties that are the most dependable, the most widely available, and the most adaptable to a wide range of climate and cultural conditions. It also includes some others that fit special conditions or special uses in the garden or landscape.

When choosing perennials for your garden, first skim through the guide, noting the plants that are particularly appealing and jotting down their names on a piece of paper. If you want plants to meet specific needs, the lists on pages 27 to 33 will help you locate them. The chart on pages 18 to 21 shows when the various plants flower and what combinations and sequences of bloom are possible.

Shasta daisies, sweet william, lilies, larkspur, ligularia, and poppies are among the many flowers flourishing in this perennial bed.

ASKING THE RIGHT QUESTIONS

The next step is to read about the plants in more detail, keeping in mind these three crucial questions.

Will this plant work? This is a question of function, whether the plant fills the intended role. Color, size, shape, texture, and bloom date should all be considered.

Will it grow in my garden? Many complex and varying factors enter into this question, but if the plant is hardy in your region, and if its requirements for soil, moisture, and light fit the conditions in your garden, then the chances of success are excellent.

Will this plant please me? This question addresses the personal tastes of the gardener. Although seemingly an obvious one, it is surprising how often this all-important criterion is overlooked in the rush of sorting through the maze of cultural instructions and opinions of others. Don't choose a plant because it fits and thrives in your garden if you don't like it.

To give as complete a picture as possible of each plant, this guide includes detailed information on physical characteristics and cultural requirements. Some of this information is of necessity very general and may need to be adjusted for specific areas. For example, bloom dates and the best times for planting and dividing vary regionally. The times given in this guide apply to USDA climate zone 6, which, as the map on page 108 shows, extends roughly on a line from Boston through Kansas City and into the Southwest. This "median" climate gives a general idea of when to expect flowers to bloom and when to plant as well as when to divide.

Bloom dates vary not only among climate zones, they can vary from year to year by days or sometimes weeks even in the same garden, depending on the weather and horticultural practices. It may be best to plant and divide a given plant in the fall in some areas and in the spring in other areas.

No one book can possibly describe how all these perennials perform in all of the diverse climatic conditions throughout the country. It's an excellent idea to double-check on how you can expect the choices made from this plant guide to do in your specific area and climate. Good sources of this information are nurseries, agricultural extension agents, universities, botanical gardens, garden clubs, and neighbors who enjoy gardening.

Beyond serving as a handy reference and a means of introducing and familiarizing yourself with the perennials, this guide can inspire further exploration into the vast and intriguing world of perennial gardening.

The key to a successful perennial border is coordinating color and bloom as effectively as in this garden where sunflowers, lilies, delphiniums, snapdragons, and campanula create a bright burst of color.

Acanthus mollis

Achillea millefolium 'Fire King'

Acanthus mollis
(A-*kan*-thus)
Bear's-breech

Acanthus family; native to the
Mediterranean region
Height: 2 feet
Spread: 4 feet
Hardy to zone 8

Bear's-breech is grown for its
clumps of immense, bold,
glossy leaves and tall flower
spikes. It is usually considered
more of a landscape plant
than a border perennial.

The dark green, deeply
lobed leaves grow to 2 feet
long, in basal clusters. The
foliage is handsome and dramatic from March to October.

The flowers are creamy
white, lavender, or rose, with
greenish or purplish bracts,
and appear along upright
stems 2 to 3 feet tall. They
bloom from late spring
through early summer.

How to start   Best planted
from divisions or nursery
plants in spring.

Where to plant   Best in
moist, rich loam with good
drainage, but does reasonably
well in dry, sandy soil. It prefers filtered shade but can

take full sun in cool climates.
It tolerates drought, but the
foliage is more lush with adequate moisture. In the northern limits of its range, plant in
a warm, protected place, and
mulch over winter. Space
plants 3 to 4 feet apart.

Care   Easy. Remove spent
flower stalks. To grow for foliage alone, remove stalks as
they appear. The roots spread
a considerable distance underground, and, like bamboo, the
plant forms spreading clumps.
Confine the roots unless you
want a large stand. Snails and
slugs may be a problem. The
plant rarely requires division
for rejuvenation but is easily
propagated by that method.
Getting all the roots is difficult, making the plant hard to
get rid of. Divide any time
from October to March.

Varieties   *Acanthus mollis*
'Latifolius' has larger leaves
and is hardier. It should be the
choice for borderline areas in
northern zone 8. *A. mollis*
'Oak Leaf' has larger leaves
that are more deeply cut, as
does *A. spinosissimus*, which
is hardy to zone 6.

Achillea filipendulina
(A-*kil*-lee-uh)
Fernleaf yarrow

Daisy family; native to Asia
Minor and the Caucasus
Height: 3 to 4 feet
Spread: 1 to 1½ feet
Hardy in all zones

The fernleaf yarrow is an easy
perennial with ferny, soft-
textured foliage and large
clusters of tiny yellow flowers.
Some excellent related species
and varieties have white or
rose-colored flowers.

The flower clusters are flat
on top and are held on elongated stalks. Bloom peaks from
late June to mid-July. Removing spent blossoms helps to
prolong the season.

The grayish foliage is
dense almost to the ground
and is effective all season. Individual plants are somewhat
open and erect, but groups of
three or more give a more
luxurious appearance.

Fernleaf yarrow is long-
lived and does not spread in-
ordinately. It occasionally
self-sows, but the seedlings
often produce inferior plants.

How to start   Plant divisions
or nursery plants in early
spring or fall. Named varieties
may not come true from seed.
Germinate indoors in Feb-
ruary or March at 65° to 70° F.
Seeds will sprout in five to
seven days. When sown outdoors in early spring, seedlings
will appear in 10 to 15 days.

Where to plant   Soil must be
well drained, preferably dry,
and of only average fertility.
Rich soil promotes weak
growth and few flowers. Give
it full sun. Yarrow tolerates
drought and poor, dry soil.
Place it away from wind to reduce the need for staking.

Care   Easy. Water only moderately, and avoid excessive
nitrogen fertilizer. Powdery
mildew and stem rot are occasional problems, especially in
moist climates. Avoid watering
late in the day. Fernleaf yarrow needs to be rejuvenated
by division every three or four
years. It propagates easily
from divisions, which should
be taken in either early fall
or spring.

Agapanthus orientalis

Alchemilla mollis

Related species and varieties *Achillea filipendulina* 'Coronation Gold' is lower growing, to 2½ or 3 feet high, blooms prolifically, and requires less staking.

A. filipendulina 'Gold Plate' has huge flower clusters, up to 6 inches across, on tall, densely foliaged 4- to 5-foot plants.

A. filipendulina 'Parkers Variety' has an open structure to 3½ feet high.

A. filipendulina 'Moonshine' is low growing, to only 1½ feet tall, with silvery foliage and pale canary yellow flowers.

A. millefolium 'Fire King' is also only 1½ feet tall, with flowers that open whitish and change to a deep rosy red. Flower clusters are 2 to 3 inches across, and leaves are more finely textured than other yarrows.

A. ptarmica 'Angels Breath' is 1 to 2 feet tall and produces great masses of tiny, double white flowers. It can be extremely invasive, especially in moist, rich soil. Divide at least every other year to restrain its growth; it may even need this annually.

Agapanthus orientalis

(Ag-a-*panth*-us)
Lily-of-the-Nile, African lily

Amaryllis family; native to South Africa
Height: 2½ to 3½ feet
Spread: 3 feet
Hardy to zone 8

This warm-season perennial is grown for its dense, rounded 6-inch heads of blue or white trumpet-shaped flowers. These are borne high above the foliage on sturdy single stalks during the summer. Each cluster can contain over one hundred blossoms, which open successively, twenty or so at a time, over a long period. The thick green leaves are strap shaped and arch out attractively from the base of the plant. The foliage is persistent, although it may die back during the winter or dry weather.

How to start Best started from nursery plants or divisions in fall or spring. Be careful not to break the thick, fleshy roots when transplanting. It can be started from seed, although it takes three years or more to produce a flowering-size plant.

Where to plant Semisunny positions are best, although it can take full sun. It prefers rich, moist, well-drained soil, although dryer conditions are well tolerated after flowering.

Care Easy, but rather slow growing. Staking is not required. It has few insect or disease problems. Divide only infrequently, as this sets the plant back. Lily-of-the-Nile is often grown as a potted plant in cooler climates and placed outdoors for the summer.

Alchemilla mollis

(Al-ke-*mill*-uh)
Lady's-mantle

Rose family; native to Europe
Height: 15 inches
Spread: 10 inches
Hardy to zone 3

Delicate, fluffy flowers arch from the refined grayish green leaves of this plant, which is useful in the front of the border or as a ground cover in partial shade.

The flowers are chartreuse or yellowish green in color and bloom from June through August. They appear on stalks up to 18 inches long.

The leaves are 3 to 4 inches wide and rounded, with lobes creased like a fan. Slightly hairy, they catch droplets of water that sparkle in the sunlight. The foliage is attractive all summer long.

Lady's-mantle is long-lived and notoriously invasive, an advantage as a ground cover.

How to start Plant divisions or nursery bedding plants in early spring or fall. Sow seed indoors in early spring at 65° F, or sow directly outdoors. Seeds germinate in eight days.

Where to plant The soil should be moist, well drained, and of average fertility. The plant prefers partial shade, especially in hot climates. Space plants 10 inches apart in clumps of three or more.

Care Easy. Keep moist. Remove spent flowers to prevent rampant spreading. There are no serious pests. Lady's-mantle can go for many years without requiring division. To increase, divide three- or four-year-old plants in fall or early spring.

Amsonia tabernaemontana

Anchusa azurea

Amsonia tabernaemontana

(Am-*sown*-e-uh)
Blue-star, amsonia

Dogbane family; native to the southeastern United States
Height: 2 to 3 feet
Spread: 1½ to 2 feet
Hardy to zone 5

Blue-star is refined and delicate, not the showiest perennial. Its clusters of small stars are effective for only two weeks in late May and early June (although in northern climates it has been known to bloom as late as July). The willowlike foliage, however, is attractive all summer long. The plant's chief advantages are that it is restrained in growth and carefree.

The flowers are an unusual steel blue in color. Tiny and delicate, they appear in dense clusters on the stems.

The foliage is bright green all summer, turning brilliant gold in the fall. The leaves are long, narrow, and medium fine in texture. The clumps of multibranched stems are bushy and semierect. The plant is very long-lived and grows slowly, never spreading too widely.

How to start Plant divisions or nursery plants in the fall. It can be grown from seed collected fresh and sown in fall. If sown in spring, prechill for several weeks, then sow at 45° F. Seeds usually sprout in three weeks.

Where to plant Blue-star performs well in nearly any soil, moist or dry, but soggy soils should be avoided. It is best in partial shade but tolerates full sun well. Space plants 12 to 15 inches apart.

Care Extremely easy. Blue-star does best with regular water and feeding. It has no serious pests. Division is rarely necessary but is an excellent means of increase. Divide in spring or fall.

Anchusa azurea

(An-*koo*-sah)
Italian bugloss, Italian alkanet

Borage family; native to the Mediterranean region
Height: 3 to 5 feet
Spread: 1½ to 2½ inches
Hardy to zone 3

Although Italian bugloss is a short-lived plant, its clouds of pure, vivid blue flowers remain in the garden for a long time because it self-sows prolifically. The striking flower color is the reason for growing this plant.

The flowers bloom in June and most of July. They are small but are borne profusely in large, loose clusters on the top third of the plant.

The foliage is dark green with bristly, hairy stems and leaves that become quite rangy and unattractive after blooming is complete. The plant is upright and spreading, with most foliage at the base.

Italian bugloss self-sows prolifically and can become a nuisance. It is often treated as a fall-sown annual or biennial, and the flowers are best on one- or two-year-old plants.

How to start Sow seed in late summer or early fall, or sow outdoors in the spring once temperatures reach 50° to 65° F. Start indoors six to eight weeks prior to the last frost in spring. Seedlings appear in 14 days.

Where to plant Italian bugloss performs well in most soils but is best in well-drained, moist loam of average to poor fertility. It prefers full sun but tolerates partial shade. Tall varieties should be located away from wind. Plant 18 to 30 inches apart.

Care Moderately easy. Water plentifully. Do not fertilize. Cut back after bloom to encourage a second, less prolific bloom. Tall varieties require staking. Crown rot is a problem in soggy soil.

Divide Italian bugloss every year or at least every other year. Thin self-sown seedlings to avoid crowding.

Varieties 'Dropmore' grows 4 to 5 feet tall with huge clouds of bright blue flowers, and needs staking. 'Loddon Royalist' reaches 3 feet in height. 'Pride of Dover' reaches 4 feet with lighter blue flowers, and requires staking. 'Royal Blue' has intense, deep blue flowers and grows to 3 feet high.

Anemone × *hybrida* 'Praecox'

Anthemis tinctoria

Anemone × hybrida

(A-*nem*-on-ee)
Japanese anemone

Buttercup family; parents
native to China, Japan,
and Nepal
Height: 2 to 5 feet
Spread: 1½ feet
Hardy to zone 6

The Japanese anemone dis-
plays attractive foliage and
loose, open clusters of flowers
in white and shades of pink.
It is especially valuable for
providing fall color in partial
shade.

The flowers are each 1½ to
3 inches across, depending on
variety and conditions of
growth, and bloom in late summer to mid-autumn.

The leaves are dark to
light green, large, and handsome; they are somewhat
reminiscent of maple leaves.
They cover the plant densely
at the bottom and become
smaller and more scarce toward the top, leaving the upper 1 to 2 feet of stem bare.
The plants slowly increase in
size and number of flowering
stems. They are long-lived in
favorable locations, and resent
disturbance once established.

How to start   Purchase
commercially produced rooted
cuttings in individual containers and plant them in
spring. To plant your own cuttings, place 2-inch pieces of
roots in sandy loam outdoors
in early spring, and keep
evenly moist.

Where to plant   Prefers
rich, moist soil high in humus.
Soil must have good drainage;
wet soil in winter is usually
fatal. The plant prefers partial
shade but tolerates full sun,
especially in cool climates.
Space plants 18 inches apart.

Care   Moderately easy. Water during dry spells in summer. In the northern limits of
its hardiness range, it is advis-
able to protect this plant with
a loose mulch, such as evergreen boughs. Do not apply
this protection until the
ground is frozen, however, or
trapped moisture could lead to
an early death. The black blis-
ter beetle can quickly defoliate
established plants.

Clumps rarely require di-
vision. If necessary, divide in
early spring; success is usually
difficult. For increase, root
cuttings are better.

Anthemis tinctoria

(*An*-them-is)
Golden marguerite

Daisy family; native to central
and southern Europe and
western Asia
Height: 2 to 3 feet
Spread: 1½ feet
Hardy to zone 3

The golden marguerite produces masses of small golden
yellow daisies on bushy
clumps in July. Although
short-lived, it is useful in the
border or for cut flowers.

The individual flowers are
small, to 2 inches in diameter,
but are massed in profusion on
long, strong stems. The plant
blooms in July, but removing
spent flowers before they set
seed can prolong the season
into September.

The fernlike leaves are
dark green on the upper surface, white and woolly on the
underside. They are medium
fine in texture, aromatic when
bruised, and effective all season long. Golden marguerite
self-sows prolifically and can
become a nuisance.

How to start   Sow seed directly outdoors in spring or
summer, or start indoors six to
eight weeks prior to setting
seedlings out after the last
frost in spring. Indoor germination will take from one to
three weeks at 68° to 70° F.
The plant often can be purchased as divisions or rooted
cuttings; plant these in spring
or early summer.

Where to plant   Golden
marguerite performs well in
nearly any well-drained soil.
Give it full sun. It tolerates
hot, dry locations and poor soil
remarkably well, but it abhors
heavy, wet, clay soils. Plant 15
to 18 inches apart.

Care   Fairly easy. Water only
moderately. There are no serious pests. Golden marguerite
must be divided at least every
other year, as clumps will die
out in the center. Annual division may be required in
moist climates. Divide in
spring or fall.

Varieties   'Moonlight' has
pale yellow flowers; 'Beauty of
Grallagh' has flowers of deep
yellow; and 'E. C. Buxton' has
very bright, yellow flowers.

Aquilegia hybrid

Armeria maritima 'Dusseldorf Pride'

Aquilegia

(Ak-wil-*ee*-jee-uh)
Columbine

Buttercup family; native to the cool northern temperate zones, mostly in North America and Europe
Height: 1½ to 3 feet
Spread: 1 to 2 feet
Hardy to zone 3

Columbines are delicate, airy plants with curiously spurred, showy flowers in a wide range of colors and forms. They are useful in the border and in "wild" or woodland gardens.

The flowers come in shades of white, blue, purple, red, pink, yellow, orange, reddish brown, or nearly black, in solids or bicolors. They appear in May and June. Hybridizers have developed a huge array of colors and flower sizes, from 1½ to 4 inches across and up to 6 inches long. The flowers nod gracefully at the ends of long, slender stems.

The foliage is light green, often with a slight silvery, dusty cast that catches and holds dewdrops. Notched, compound leaves give the plant an open, fine-textured appearance rather like that of maidenhair fern. The foliage can be effective into August. The plant grows from 1½ to 3 feet tall.

Columbine is usually short-lived, especially if the soil does not have perfect drainage. It does self-sow in favorable environments, but the offspring will differ, often radically, from hybrid parents.

How to start Can be started from seed, although young seedlings or divisions from a nursery are the usual methods. Sow seed outdoors in early spring or summer for flowers the next year. Or start indoors in a flat of sandy soil 12 to 14 weeks before setting out in midspring. Refrigerate the flat for three weeks, then put it in a moist, shady place at 70° to 75° F. Do not cover the seeds. Germination usually occurs in three to four weeks.

Where to plant These are predominantly woodland plants and, as such, prefer cool, moist soil rich in organic matter. Drainage must be excellent. They prefer filtered shade but can take full sun in cool-summer climates. Space plants 1 to 2 feet apart.

Care Moderately difficult unless species are grown. Water generously and give regular light feedings. The chief pest problem is disfigurement of foliage by leafminers or columbine borers. Spray with malathion in early, middle, and late May. Remove infected plants.

Division can be performed for increase in August and September, but it is better to keep new plants coming on by sowing fresh seed yearly. When dividing, perform the operation quickly. Never allow the roots to dry out.

Armeria maritima

(Ar-*meer*-ee-uh)
Sea-pink, sea-thrift

Leadwort family; native to the seacoasts of Europe, Asia Minor, and northern Africa
Height: 4 inches to 2 feet, depending on species
Spread: 1 to 1½ feet
Hardy to zone 3

The sea-pink is a hardy evergreen perennial that forms dense cushions of grasslike foliage from which arise small, rounded flowers in colors of white or pale pink to deep rose. The plant is excellent for edging, rock gardens, cut flowers, and possibly for beds and borders.

The flowers appear in May and June and sporadically the year around in mild climates. They are produced in dense, tiny heads about 1 inch in diameter atop erect stems reaching 6 to 12 inches above the foliage.

The leaves make a low mound 3 or 4 inches high, but the size is variable from seed. The mounds gradually expand by short runners into clumps 1 to 1½ feet across. After about four years (sooner in very moist locations) the center begins to die out, necessitating division.

How to start Young plants are often sold in flats or containers as divisions, but they are easy to start from seed. Soak the seeds for several hours and then sow outdoors in spring or summer. Or start indoors by sowing seed in a

Artemisia schmidtiana

Aruncus dioicus

flat of sandy soil and maintaining a temperature of 65° to 70° F. Germination occurs in two to three weeks.

Where to plant   Sea-pink must have excellent drainage and performs well in almost pure sand. It is best in dry, infertile soil and full sun. It takes constant wind and salt spray beautifully. Space plants 6 to 12 inches apart.

Care   Easy. Do not fertilize except in the poorest of soils, and then only lightly. Water moderately. Too much moisture and rich soil hasten dying out in the center. Prolong bloom by removing faded flowers. Do not mulch over the winter, or rot may result. The plant has no serious pests.

When the center of the clump begins to die, divide to rejuvenate. Division is an excellent means of increase and can be done in spring, summer, or fall.

Related species and varieties   Sea-pink is quite variable from seed, and many cultivars are listed. Where uniformity of size or color is desired, it is best to choose a named variety.

Armeria plantaginea is like a large *A. maritima*, growing 1½ to 2 feet tall. Although it is less frequently available commercially, its larger size suits it better to the border. Like *A. maritima*, it is extremely variable from seed. 'Bee's Ruby' has later, bright, deep red flowers in June and July.

Artemisia schmidtiana 'Silver Mound'

(Ar-tem-*is*-ee-uh)
Wormwood, silver mound, angel's hair

Daisy family; native to Japan
Height: 1 foot
Spread: 1½ feet
Hardy to zone 5

Wormwood is famous for its intense silvery gray, feathery foliage produced in neat, dense mounds.

The leaves are heavily divided, have a very soft, fine texture, and form a bushy, rounded mound. The flowers are inconspicuous.

Wormwood is usually long-lived, but if the soil is too

moist, particularly during winter, it does not survive long. If the soil is too rich, the foliage tends to become too lush and the plant will open at the center instead of mounding nicely. It never spreads or reseeds.

How to start   Stem cuttings are easy to root during the summer; most nursery plants are started this way. Set young plants out in spring.

Where to plant   Wormwood must have fast drainage; it will not tolerate soggy roots, especially in winter. Poor, dry, sandy soil and full sun are best. It takes heat but is prone to rot in humid climates. Space plants 18 to 24 inches apart.

Care   Easy. Avoid overwatering or fertilizing. Rust is the only serious pest, but fungicide is rarely required. Always water early in the day, and avoid letting water stand on the foliage for any length of time. Division is difficult, never necessary, and seldom successful.

Related species and varieties   *Artemisia absinthium* 'Powys Castle' (Powys Castle wormwood) is a classic in the border for its pale

leaves. *A. ludoviciana* (silver king artemisia) grows to 3 feet and has white leaves. Divide yearly to control spread.

Aruncus dioicus

(formerly *A. sylvester*)
(A-*runk*-us)
Goatsbeard

Rose family; native to Eurasia and North America
Height: 5 to 7 feet
Spread: 3 to 5 feet
Hardy to zone 4

Goatsbeard is a large, shrublike perennial that produces showy, silky white plumes in midsummer. The plant suggests a huge *Astilbe* and is excellent in partial shade in the rear of the border or as a shrub accent, particularly in combination with *Astilbe* and *Filipendula*.

The flowers are minute and gathered into the gracefully relaxed plumes, which are often as long as 16 inches. Goatsbeard blooms from mid-June to early July.

The foliage is medium green with large, compound leaves of bold texture. It is effective all season long.

Asclepias tuberosa

Aster sinensis

Goatsbeard is long-lived and, despite its large size, restrained in growth and not invasive.

How to start Seeds sown at 45° F in early spring germinate in two weeks. Only male plants have the feathery white plumes that are so striking; female plants have hard, greenish flowers that are interesting but not nearly as dramatic. Set container-grown plants out in early spring.

Where to plant Needs moist, preferably rich soil high in organic matter. Goatsbeard is best grown in partial shade, such as under a high canopy of trees or on the east side of a building. With sufficient moisture it tolerates full sun. Space plants 3 to 5 feet apart.

Care Easy. Water generously and deeply. Fertilize regularly during the growing season. Despite its height, it never needs staking. It has no serious pests. The plant can go many years before needing division for rejuvenation. Division for increase is difficult and not often successful.

Asclepias tuberosa
(As-*klee*-pee-as)
Butterfly flower,
butterfly weed

Milkweed family; native from New England to North Dakota, south to Florida, Arizona, and New Mexico
Height: 1½ to 3 feet
Spread: 1 to 1½ feet
Hardy to zone 3

The brilliant orange-red clusters of flowers that appear on this North American native in midsummer attract hordes of butterflies, hummingbirds, and bees.

The flowers may be deep orange, pale lemon, or deep, oxblood red. The tiny blooms occur in dense clusters. Butterfly flower blooms from June to August, with peak bloom from mid-June to early July. The milkweedlike fruits are attractive in dried arrangements.

The lance-shaped leaves are dark green and hairy. Each plant is composed of a cluster of erect stems branched toward the top spreading form. The plant is restrained in growth and long-lived. Its deep taproot makes it drought tolerant but also

makes it difficult to divide or transplant.

How to start It is best to plant the tuberous bare roots in the fall or early spring. Set the bare taproot vertically into the soil with the eye 1 to 2 inches below the soil. Seed germination is erratic and unpredictable. Sow seed outdoors in May or indoors in early spring at 68° to 75° F. Seedlings appear in three to four weeks.

Where to plant Native to meadows and prairies, butterfly flower does best in light, sandy, poor soil and full sun. Still, it does well in peaty soil or even heavy clay. Avoid excessively moist soils. It tolerates wind. Space plants 12 to 18 inches apart.

Care Easy. Water only through drought, especially in heavy soils. Butterfly flower is slow to appear in the spring, so take care when cultivating around its area; it's wise to mark its place. There are no serious pests. Division is never necessary; in fact, it's difficult and seldom successful.

Aster
(*As*-ter)
Hardy aster, michaelmas daisy

Daisy family; the parents of many hybrids are native to North America, Europe, and Asia
Height: 9 inches to 6 feet, depending on species
Spread: 1 to 1½ feet
Hardy to zone 4

Asters produce daisylike flowers in late summer and fall in every color but orange. Many varieties are available for different flower colors and sizes. Although requiring frequent division, they are easy to grow.

The flowers are usually violet-purple or blue, but many shades of purple, red, pink, and white are also available. All have yellow centers. They are about 2 inches across and are produced in large clusters. Asters bloom any time from August into October, depending upon the variety.

The foliage is dark to dusty green and of medium texture. Low-growing varieties are bushy, prostrate, and spreading, creating dense carpets of

Astilbe 'Gloria Purpurea'

color as low as 9 inches. Taller varieties range from 1½ feet to 6 feet high, and their clusters of erect stems are heavily branched toward the top and densely covered with foliage.

The aster form is generally upright and spreading. Clumps increase quickly and begin to die out in the center at an early age, necessitating division. The plant reseeds sporadically, but the hybrids do not breed true to type. It is usually short-lived.

How to start Named varieties are best started by divisions, nursery plants, or hand-pollinated seed. Set out divisions or young plants in early spring. Sow seed outdoors in spring or early summer, or indoors in early spring. Sow thickly, as the percentage of germination is usually low. Seedlings appear in two to three weeks at 70° to 75° F.

Where to plant Asters are not too particular about soil, but light, moist, well-drained soil of average fertility is best. They accept full sun or partial shade, preferring the latter in hot southern climates. Space plants 12 to 20 inches apart.

Care Moderately easy to moderately difficult. The plant performs best with abundant water, but never allow roots to remain soggy. Feed only lightly. Pinch in late spring to produce better flowering and denser plants. Varieties over 2 feet tall need staking.

Rust and powdery mildew can be serious, so protect plants throughout the growing season with a weekly spraying of a fungicide. It helps to keep foliage dry in cool weather or in the evening. Japanese beetles can also be a problem, particularly on early-blooming varieties. Late-blooming flowers usually open after the beetle season has run its course.

Division is necessary at least every other year, and often annually, as clumps start dying out in the center. Division is an excellent means of increase and should be done in early spring.

Related species and varieties *Aster × frikartii* 'Wonder of Stafa' is the best choice for the hot, humid summers of the Southeast. Its lavender-blue flowers sometimes appear as early as June

and still bloom well into October. It is marginally hardy in southern zone 6. Mulch well in the northern limits of its range to protect over winter. It grows 2½ feet tall and needs staking.

Astilbe
(As-*til*-be)
Meadowsweet, false-spirea

Saxifrage family; native to eastern Asia
Height: 1 to 2 feet
Spread: 1 to 2 feet
Hardy to zone 4

Meadowsweet is a favorite perennial for shady, moist locations. It also performs well in full sun. It has glossy, dark green foliage and fluffy plumes of white, pink, lavender, or red flowers on erect or arching stems. The tiny flowers are produced in great quantities, and the effect is delicate and feathery. It blooms in June and July.

The leaves are divided and compound. Sometimes tinged with bronze, they resemble ferns, and are always lush and refined. The foliage forms

bushy mounds rarely exceeding 1 or 2 feet in height; the flowers often reach another 12 to 18 inches higher.

Meadowsweet spreads gradually as clumps expand. Being a heavy feeder, it depletes the soil and thus flowers less as years go by, but division every three or four years rejuvenates it. The plant is restrained in growth, not invasive, and long-lived.

How to start Divisions or nursery plants are best set out in spring. Nurseries frequently offer young container-grown plants. Seed is difficult to germinate and is radically variable.

Where to plant Prefers a cool, moist location in light shade, with deep, rich soil high in organic matter. Meadowsweet does not tolerate wet winters well without adequate drainage and will not take summer drought. It performs well in deep shade but accepts full sun if watered deeply and often. Space plants 1 to 2 feet apart.

Care Moderately easy. Give generous applications of 5-10-10 fertilizer each spring

Aurinia saxatilis

Baptisia australis

just as growth begins. Water abundantly. Japanese beetles can be a serious pest. Powdery mildew, slugs, and snails also can be problems. Although the plant performs adequately without division, for maximum flower size and quantity, divide it every three or four years. It is easy to propagate by dividing the rootstock just as plants are beginning to grow in the spring.

Aurinia saxatilis
(formerly *Alyssum saxatile*)
(Oh-*rin*-ee-uh)
Basket-of-gold, goldentuft

Mustard family; native to southern and central Europe and Turkey
Height: 9 to 12 inches
Spread: 12 to 15 inches
Hardy to zone 3

Basket-of-gold is a low, bushy perennial of variable habit, covered with bright, lemon yellow flowers in April and May. Useful in dry, poor soil, it is frequently grown in rock gardens.

The tiny flowers are produced in tremendous profusion, entirely covering the plant. The foliage is gray-green, providing an interesting accent when the plant is not in bloom. The leaves are small, elongated, and dense.

The form varies according to the selected variety and the growth conditions. In rich, moist soil it tends to be open and sprawling; in dry, poor soil it is compact and bushy. It is fairly short-lived.

How to start Plant divisions or nursery plants in early spring, or sow seed outdoors in early spring. Seedlings appear in one to two weeks.

Where to plant Dry, poor, infertile soil in full sun is preferred, and drainage must be excellent. Plant 8 to 12 inches apart.

Care Water only moderately through periods of drought. Do not fertilize. After blooming is over, cut the stems to half their length to keep the plant vigorous. It has no serious pests. Divide to increase in spring just as growth commences.

Baptisia australis
(Bap-*tiz*-ee-a)
False-indigo

Pea family; native from Pennsylvania south to North Carolina and Tennessee
Height: 3 to 4 feet
Spread: 3 to 4 feet
Hardy to zone 3

False-indigo is hardy, pest free, undemanding, and one of the easiest perennials to grow. It is excellent for backgrounds, at the rear of the border, or as a shrublike mass in the landscape.

The flowers are often described as indigo blue, but they actually range from pale lavender to dark purple. They are pea shaped, about 1 inch long, and are produced in long, erect spikes at the tops of the branches, appearing in late May to early June.

The foliage is dense, lush, and remains attractive until hard frost in the fall. The cloverlike leaves are a clean, bright green and are divided into three leaflets. The first frost turns the foliage a dramatic black, creating a strong sculptural effect until the first snow knocks it down.

False-indigo forms shrubby, rounded masses 3 to 4 feet tall, sometimes taller, and spreads as wide. It is restrained in growth, will not spread, and is long-lived.

How to start Best from young nursery plants. It is easy to grow from seed sown outdoors in late fall or early spring, but it will not begin to flower for two or three years. Propagating from division is difficult.

Where to plant Best in well-drained garden loam of average fertility. It tolerates almost all but very wet soils. Give it full sun or partial shade, although it flowers less in shade. Plant 18 to 24 inches apart.

Care Extremely easy. The tallest plants may require staking. Remove spent flowers to prolong bloom. (The black, long-lasting seedpods are, however, considered attractive by many.) Like other legumes, it fixes its own nitrogen from the atmosphere and needs little if any feeding. It prefers poor soil. Water only moderately.

Belamcanda chinensis

Bergenia cordifolia

Although powdery mildew and rust are reported, they are seldom serious problems. Division is extremely difficult due to the deep taproot, and is seldom successful. Luckily, it is not necessary either for rejuvenation or propagation.

Belamcanda chinensis

(Bel-am-*can*-da)
Blackberry-lily, leopard-flower

Iris family; native to China and Japan
Height: 2 to 4 feet
Spread: 1 to 3 feet
Hardy to zone 5

Blackberry-lily produces great quantities of star-shaped flowers in late July and August. Orange with red dots, the flowers measure about 2 inches across and appear on multibranched stems that can reach as high as 4 feet. The seed clusters are attractive in dried arrangements.

The swordlike leaves are bright green to gray-green and resemble those of tall bearded iris. They form large clumps.

Blackberry-lily may reseed, but the seedlings are easy to weed out. The clumps expand slowly, and are long-lived.

How to start   Easy to start from seed, but faster results occur from nursery plants or tubers divided and planted in the spring.

Where to plant   Blackberry-lily must have well-drained soil; winter sogginess is usually fatal. Give it full sun. Space plants 1 to 3 feet apart. The plant is best used, however, as a single specimen.

Care   Easy in well-drained soil. In northern areas it should be mulched in winter. Iris borer can be a severe pest. See *Iris* (bearded iris) for recommendations. Although division is an excellent method for increase, clumps can go for many years without needing it. Division is best done in spring or early fall.

Related species   *Belamcanda flabellata* is similar in all respects except that the flowers are clear yellow and bloom slightly later, into September. It is less commonly available.

Bergenia cordifolia

(Ber-*geen*-ee-uh)
Bergenia, heartleaf bergenia

Saxifrage family; native to Siberia and Mongolia
Height: 12 to 15 inches
Spread: 12 to 18 inches
Hardy to zone 2

Bergenia is a low-growing evergreen perennial with large, cabbagelike leaves and pink or white flowers. Undemanding, adaptable to nearly any situation, and extremely hardy, it is useful in the front of the border or massed as a bed or ground cover.

The flowers are about ¾ inch wide and appear in clusters atop stems extending 6 to 12 inches above the foliage. They normally bloom in April and May, but flowers may not appear in areas of severe winters or other harsh exposure.

The foliage is medium green in summer, with a reddish tinge in winter. Leaves are wavy edged, fleshy, and measure 10 inches across, radiating in all directions from the base.

Bergenia spreads by rhizomes that creep along the soil surface, forming dense mats of leaves. It grows slowly and is never invasive.

How to start   Although best started from divisions in early spring, bergenia also grows from seed sown outdoors in late fall or early spring.

Where to plant   Bergenia tolerates a wide variety of soils, performing well in poor, dry ones and rich, moist ones, but it prefers well-drained soil of average fertility. More frequent division is necessary in rich, moist soil. Give it either sun or shade. Shade is better in hot-summer regions. Space plants 12 to 18 inches apart.

Care   Easy. It responds vigorously to fertilizing, but this results in bare spots and the need for more frequent division. Water only moderately for the same reason. It has no serious pests but does provide a haven for snails. On dry sites with relatively infertile soil, it does not need division for years. In rich, moist soil it may need dividing about every four years.

Boltonia asteroides

Brunnera macrophylla

Boltonia asteroides

(Bowl-*to*-nee-uh)
Boltonia, false-chamomile

Daisy family; native to eastern
North America
Height: 3 to 5 feet
Spread: 3 feet
Hardy to zone 4

Boltonia bears numerous
daisylike flowers on branching
stems from late summer to
October. The ¾-inch flowers
range in color from white to
purplish. Each bloom has a
bright yellow central disk. The
plant is bushy, with numerous
narrow, blue-green leaves that
also line the flower stalks. It
makes an excellent cut flower.

How to start Plant divisions
or nursery plants in early
spring or after blooming in
fall. Space them 3 feet apart.

Where to plant Prefers rich
soil, although average soil is
acceptable. It tolerates both
moist and dry soils, although
flowering is heavier where
moisture is abundant. Full to
dappled sun is best. It is best
grown in the back of the border because of its large size
and late flowering season.

Care This easy-to-grow plant
has retained all the toughness
of its wild ancestors and can
basically be left to fend for itself. In spite of its height, no
staking is usually required. It
is susceptible to mildew.

Brunnera macrophylla

(*Brun*-er-uh)
Siberian bugloss

Borage family; native to the
Caucasus and western Siberia
Height: 12 inches
Spread: 12 to 18 inches
Hardy to zone 3

The tiny flowers of Siberian
bugloss, produced in delicate
clusters, resemble those of
Anchusa azurea, the Italian
bugloss. This plant, however,
has the advantage of excellent
large, heart-shaped leaves that
remain attractive all season.

The flowers are a clear sky
blue, and bloom on stems 12
to 15 inches tall. They bloom
from April through May and
resemble forget-me-nots.

The dark green leaves are
clean, lush, and pest free.

They reach 6 to 8 inches long
in July and grow in clumps
about 12 inches high. There is
also a variegated form. The foliage is attractive until frost.

The plant expands outward
gradually. It is well behaved
and lives a long time without
requiring division.

How to start Take clump divisions in early spring, purchase nursery plants, or sow
seed outdoors in early fall. To
sow seed in spring, freeze for
one week; then sow in early
spring at 45° F. Germination
takes two weeks.

Where to plant Exceedingly
adaptable, the plant does well
in any soil, in sun or shade.
Like most garden plants, however, it responds to a moist soil
high in organic matter. Partial
shade is best. Space plants 12
to 18 inches apart.

Care Easy. It prefers abundant water and regular feeding but does well with little
attention. It has no serious
pests. Division is needed if the
center begins to die out, but it
is usually many years before
this occurs.

Caltha palustris

(*Kal*-tha)
Marshmarigold

Buttercup family; native to
Europe, Asia, and North Amer-
ica from Alaska to North
Carolina
Height: 12 to 18 inches
Spread: 12 to 24 inches
Hardy to zone 3

The marshmarigold is a cheer-
ful plant for wet, soggy soil or
standing water. It has bright
golden yellow flowers about 1
inch across borne singly above
the foliage. The bright green,
rounded leaves are held horizontally on tall, juicy stems. A
spring bloomer (May), it disappears by midsummer.

The plant is fairly low
growing, from 12 to 18 inches
high. Although not considered
invasive, it spreads to form
loose clumps and mats. It reseeds if conditions are
favorable.

How to start Divisions and
nursery plants are best. To
grow from seed, sow only fresh
seed in pots, plunge the pots in
water to just below the rim,

Caltha palustris 'Multiplex'

Campanula glomerata

Campanula lactiflora

and then keep the surface evenly moist. Plants bloom the third year from seed.

Where to plant Rich soil high in organic matter with a constant supply of moisture is best. With sufficient watering the plant tolerates dry soils. It grows happily in marshy areas or standing water. Give it full sun or very light shade. Plant 12 to 24 inches apart.

Care Moderately easy to moderately difficult. Water abundantly and fertilize regularly. Mulch well if it is planted in exposed, dry locations. There are no serious pests. Divide to increase just after blooming is over. The plant can go for years without needing division.

Campanula persicifolia

(Kam-*pan*-ew-la)
Peachleaf bellflower

Harebell family; native to Europe and northeastern Asia
Height: 2 to 3 feet
Spread: 1½ feet
Hardy to zone 3

The dainty blue or white single or double flowers of the peachleaf bellflower are bell shaped and 1½ inches in diameter. They are borne in July in sprays held well above the foliage. The strap-shaped medium green leaves may be evergreen in warmer climates.

How to start Best grown from nursery plants or divisions made in early spring. It can also be grown from spring-sown seed, although considerable variety in height and flower colors will result from seed-grown plants.

Where to plant Grows best in moist, well-drained soil. Add compost or peat moss at planting time. Full sun to light shade is best in the North; protect it from midday sun in warmer climates. Space plants 12 to 18 inches apart.

Care Easy. Water as needed to prevent wilting. Staking is not usually required. Remove flower stems in midsummer to encourage reblooming. Divide every three to four years in spring or whenever overcrowding causes clumps to decline. Susceptible to crown rot in overly moist conditions.

Related species *Campanula carpatica* (Carpathian harebell) is a low, 6- to 12-inch-high plant with large blue, purple, or white flowers from June to August. It is compact, long blooming, and useful in the rock garden or as an edging. Protect from slugs.

C. glomerata (clustered bellflower, danesblood bellflower) bears very dense clusters of ¾- to 1-inch flowers in shades of blue, purple, and white on a 1- to 3-foot plant. Blooms in early summer and again late in the season.

C. lactiflora (milky bellflower) bears white to pale blue 1-inch flowers on showy spikes to 4 feet high. It prefers moist, fertile soil and requires staking.

C. pyramidalis (chimney bellflower) is a tall-growing (5-foot), short-lived perennial with blue to white flowers on a narrow stalk, which may require staking. It can be used as a substitute for delphiniums where the latter do not grow well. It self-seeds readily, but not to the point of becoming a nuisance.

C. rapunculoides (rover bellflower) bears nodding violet-purple 1-inch flowers on 3-foot stalks. The toothed leaves are heart shaped at the base of the plant narrowing to a lance shape near the flower spike. Remove the flowers after blooming, and contain the plant within a barrier to prevent excessive spread through seeds and rhizomes. This can become a pest where conditions are ideal, but always an attractive pest. It might be best to sink it in pots. It makes a lovely cut flower.

Catananche caerulea

(Kat-a-*nan*-ke)
Cupid's-dart

Daisy family; native to southern Europe
Height: 2 feet
Spread: 1 foot
Hardy to zone 5

The lavender-blue or white daisylike flowers of Cupid's-dart appear in July and measure 2 inches in diameter. Their lacy appearance comes from the notch in the tip of each ray flower. Each is borne singly on a narrow stem well above the basal rosette of narrow, grayish green leaves.

Catananche caerulea

Ceratostigma plumbaginoides

How to start Can be grown from divisions in spring or fall or from seed sown outdoors in early spring. It may bloom the first year from seed.

Where to plant Plant in full sun in well-drained, even dry, soil. Space 12 inches apart.

Care Easy. Feed lightly and infrequently. Avoid soils that remain moist during the winter, as it is very susceptible to rot. Cupid's-dart may be short-lived, so divide or resow regularly. It is an excellent cut flower, fresh or dried.

Ceratostigma plumbaginoides

(Ser-at-*os*-tig-ma)
Blue plumbago

Leadwort family; native to western Asia
Height: 6 to 10 inches
Spread: 18 inches
Hardy to zone 6 but performs well in zone 5 with a light winter mulch

The blue plumbago is a low-growing, leafy perennial with brilliant gentian blue flowers in late summer. Its late-season blue makes it an excellent

choice for beds, edging, and the front of the border.

The flowers are bright blue upon opening and change to violet as they age. They appear in great quantities, completely covering the plant, from August to frost.

The dark green leaves often turn a bronzy red in cool fall weather. Foliage is dense and of medium to fine texture. Masses of slender, almost prostrate stems radiate from the center, sending up many short, vertical stems, each bearing flowers.

The plant spreads slowly by underground stems; in sand, the spread is rapid. It is long-lived and not invasive. Division is rarely required. Growth is slow to appear in spring, so be cautious with early cultivation.

How to start Transplant nursery plants or clumps divided in early spring.

Where to plant Although not too particular about soil, the plant does best in well-drained, moist soil high in organic matter. Avoid excessively soggy or dry soils. Give it full sun or partial shade. It

is highly tolerant of drought. Space 12 to 18 inches apart.

Care Blue plumbago requires little attention but will respond to abundant moisture and regular fertilizing. It has no serious pests. It rarely needs division, but clumps may start to die out in the center after three or four years. This is easily corrected by division. Best performed in early spring, division is also an excellent means of increase.

Chrysanthemum hybrids

(Kri-*santh*-em-um)
Hardy chrysanthemum

Daisy family; of hybrid origin
Height: 1 to 4 feet
Spread: 1½ to 2 feet
Hardy to zone 6, possibly to zone 5 with excellent drainage

Difficult to grow well, hardy chrysanthemums nevertheless can provide an outstanding show when nearly all other perennials have gone dormant for the winter. The plants offer an amazing variety of colors, sizes, and flower shapes. For the gardener with

patience and time to devote to them, they yield extraordinary late-season dividends.

Chrysanthemums come in all colors except blue. Most varieties are fully double, with two flowers 2 to 4 inches across (and usually larger with disbudding, described later), produced alone or in clusters at the ends of branched stems. Some of the many forms available are described here.

Decorative chrysanthemums have fully double flowers with straplike "petals" or, more accurately, rays.

Pompons produce rounded, almost spherical flowers usually 2 inches or less across.

Singles are daisylike with an outer single or double row of rays and an often contrasting central eye.

Cushions usually have double flowers and are distinguished by their low, bushy habit, rarely exceeding 15 inches in height.

Spoons are odd-shaped flowers with long rays flaring out into spoonlike tips.

Commercials are grown primarily by commercial growers in greenhouses and are

Chrysanthemum 'Loyalty'

Chrysanthemum coccineum 'Brenda'

characterized by the popular, huge "football" mums.

Anemones have contrasting outer rays and inner, fluffy eyes.

Buttons are like tiny pompoms an inch or less across.

Rayonettes have a spidery, open quality with long, filamentous rays. They are often called spider mums.

Hardy chrysanthemums bloom any time from August to November, depending upon the variety, and may bloom into December in mild climates.

The plant's overall structure differs according to the variety, but generally is a cluster of many-branched stems. Forms range from the low, spreading cushion mums to tall, narrow, upright ones. Heights range from 1 to 4 feet. The foliage is deep green, usually dense, and attractive unless damaged by pests.

The plants gradually expand outward. They are restrained in growth, and can be long-lived if properly cared for.

How to start Division or stem cuttings made in late spring are the best methods. Do not set out young plants too early if a tall habit is not desired.

Where to plant Rich, fertile soil high in organic matter is best, and it is critical that the soil be perfectly drained in winter. Once established, the plants can withstand mild drought. They flower best in full sun, but usually accept partial shade well. Space plants 18 to 24 inches apart.

Care Difficult for best appearance. Tip-pinching from spring to mid-summer results in bushier, more heavily flowered plants. Start when the spring growth reaches about 6 inches, and continue each time it grows another 6 inches until mid- to late July. Tall plants may need staking at flowering time. Feed regularly and generously throughout the growing season. Water regularly, especially over dry periods. Protect over winter with a 3- or 4-inch cover of mulch, placed after the ground is completely frozen. Chrysanthemums rot quickly in cold, soggy soil. To achieve fewer but larger show-quality flowers, gardeners practice disbudding. Remove all but four or five of the strongest stems in each clump, and when buds begin to show, pinch off all except the one at the top.

A wide range of pests can attack chrysanthemums. Regular spraying with an all-purpose spray (containing both an insecticide and a fungicide) and good garden sanitation are essential for healthy plants. Carefully remove and destroy any plants infected with aster yellows, foliar nematodes, and stunting (a viral disease).

Most varieties require annual division to retain vigor and good appearance, although some can get by with division every other year. Dividing is best done in spring.

Chrysanthemum coccineum

(Kri-*santh*-em-um)
Painted daisy, pyrethrum

Daisy family; native to southwestern Asia
Height: 9 inches to 3 feet, depending on variety
Spread: 1 to 1½ feet
Hardy to zone 2

The painted daisy is much easier to cultivate than the hardy chrysanthemum and blooms earlier, from June to early July. It has daisylike flowers in intense colors of red, pink, and white, often with a contrasting eye.

The flowers are 2 to 3 inches across and are produced at the ends of long stems. They may be single or double.

The bright green, deeply dissected leaves are finely textured but relatively sparse. Stems are upright to spreading and frequently branched. Painted daisies form clumps that gradually increase by sending up new shoots on the outer perimeter of the crown. They are long-lived and not invasive.

How to start Purchase nursery plants, or start by division in late summer.

Where to plant Needs reasonably well-drained soil high in organic matter. A rich, sandy loam is best. It will not tolerate wet soil in winter. Give it full sun or very light shade. Space plants 12 to 18 inches apart.

Care Moderately easy. Painted daisy tolerates moderate drought but does best

Chrysanthemum parthenium

Chrysanthemum × superbum

with sufficient water. It seldom needs staking. Cut all stems to the ground after flowering to encourage a secondary bloom in late summer. There are no serious pests. Division is usually necessary to relieve crowding after the fourth year, and is best done in late summer. After dividing and transplanting the clump, trim the leaves in half to reduce wilting. Division is an excellent means of increase.

Chrysanthemum parthenium

(Kri-*santh*-em-um)
Feverfew, matricaria

Daisy family; native to southeastern Europe and the Caucasus
Height: 12 to 15 inches
Spread: 12 to 24 inches
Hardy to zone 4

Small, daisylike flowers in incredible profusion cover these low, bushy plants in July and August. White with yellow centers, the blooms come in single- and double-flowered forms.

The flowers measure from ½ to ¾ inch in diameter and appear at the ends of multi-branched stems. The leaves are light green, small, dense, and pleasantly fragrant. Some varieties have golden leaves. In mild climates the foliage is evergreen.

Feverfew is a low, spreading plant. Most named varieties grow 12 to 15 inches high. Seedlings can, however, eventually reach 3 feet and sprawl in an open fashion unless pinched or sheared early in the season. Single-flowered forms will self-sow invasively; the double-flowered varieties are less prolific. The species is quite long-lived, unlike the double-flowered cultivars.

How to start   Seed sown in spring will produce flowering plants that summer. It is also easy to grow by cuttings or divisions. In fact, the smallest piece of root taken inadvertently by a spade will start a new (sometimes unwanted) plant.

Where to plant   Feverfew tolerates many soils but performs best in sandy, well-drained loam. Give it full sun, although it is quite tolerant of partial shade. Space plants 12 to 24 inches apart.

Care   Easy, except for removing unwanted seedlings. Pinch in spring to produce denser, bushier plants. The reseeding problem makes it tempting to try removing flowers before they can set seed, but this is nearly impossible, as there are so many blossoms, and new ones are always appearing. The plant has no serious pests. Division is seldom if ever required for rejuvenation but is good for propagation in early spring.

Chrysanthemum × superbum

(Kri-*santh*-em-um)
Shasta daisy

Daisy family; of hybrid origin, the parents are probably native to Portugal and the Pyrenees
Height: 2 to 4 feet
Spread: 2 to 4 feet
Hardy to zone 5

White, daisylike flowers with a contrasting yellow eye generously cover this bushy plant all summer long.

The blossoms are 2 to 3 inches across and are produced in great profusion at the ends of strong stems. They bloom from June to frost. Single and double varieties are available.

The dark green leaves are narrow, toothed, and almost linear in shape. About an inch long, they are held close to the stem, presenting a fine texture. The plant is densely branched, rounded, and bushy. The foliage often persists well into winter, and the plant is grown as an evergreen perennial in mild climates, where it tends to become woody at the base.

The Shasta daisy is restrained in growth and can be long-lived, given the right location and proper care.

How to start   Best planted as a nursery plant or division in spring. Sowing seed in spring is possible and easy, but will result in considerable variation in plants.

Where to plant   Moist, fertile, very well-drained soil is best. It will not tolerate soggy soil in winter. Provide good air circulation and either full sun or partial shade. The double varieties show a distinct preference for partial shade in hot climates. Space plants 12 to 24 inches apart.

Cimicifuga racemosa

Chrysogonum virginianum

Care   Moderately easy. Water generously, especially during drought. It responds favorably to occasional feeding. Removing spent flowers encourages heavier bloom. Leaf spot, stem rot, verticillium rot, and several chewing insects can be troublesome. Plants attacked by verticillium rot should be carefully removed and destroyed. Division is usually necessary every other year to restore vigor. It is best done in the spring.

Chrysogonum virginianum
(Kris-*og*-o-num)
Goldenstar

Daisy family; native from Pennsylvania to Florida and Louisiana
Height: 2 to 4 inches
Spread: 12 to 20 inches
Hardy to zones 5 and 6

Goldenstar is a low, trailing plant with small, daisylike, bright yellow flowers and vivid green leaves. It is useful either in sun or shade, and is particularly delightful when grown against or around rocks.

The flowers appear in mid-June to frost and are produced along the joints of trailing, leafy stems. The leaves are small and round, and are densely produced. Most varieties sold commercially have gray-green foliage.

The plant has a loose, open habit. It usually grows 2 to 4 inches high, and rarely exceeds 8 inches. It often spreads into a loose mat with stems rooting where they touch the soil. Goldenstar is always restrained in growth and never invasive.

How to start   Best started in early spring from divisions or nursery plants. It can be started from seed sown in late spring or late summer, but expect considerable variation in leaf size and leaf color.

Where to plant   Goldenstar must have excellent drainage and prefers a sandy soil high in organic matter. Give it either full sun or partial shade. The soil should be fairly dry and of only average fertility. Space plants 8 to 12 inches apart.

Care   Moderately easy. Removing spent flowers before

they set seed prolongs flowering. Water moderately during periods of drought. There are no serious pests. Divide in early spring for increase. The plant does not require division for rejuvenation.

Cimicifuga racemosa
(Si-mi-*siff*-yew-ga)
Bugbane, black snakeroot

Buttercup family; native from Massachusetts to Ontario, south to Georgia, Tennessee, and Missouri
Height: 2 to 3 feet
Spread: 2 feet
Hardy to zone 3

Bugbane produces tall, thin, exceedingly graceful spires of white, fluffy flowers, sometimes reaching to 8 feet above the foliage clumps. It is excellent at the rear of the border.

Open and airy in bloom, the wandlike flower stalks sway with each breeze. The flowers are small and are produced densely, covering the upper 2 to 3 feet of the stalks.

They are vertical and graceful and exude a cloyingly sweet fragrance. The peak bloom occurs in late June and

July, but small lateral branches bear flowers into August.

The glistening, dark green leaves are compound, divided into three toothed leaflets. The foliage forms dense clumps and provides good color until frost.

Bugbane does not self-sow freely or spread about the garden and can never be considered invasive. The rhizomes expand slowly into clumps. The plant is very long-lived.

How to start   Best done by dividing in early spring or planting nursery plants with well-developed root systems. To plant a bare-root clump from a division, place the rhizome (one with at least two eyes) so that the eyes are exactly 1 inch below soil level. Seeds can be collected and sown in the fall. To sow in spring, prechill the seeds in the refrigerator for several weeks. Sow at 45° to 50° F. Germination is slow and erratic.

Where to plant   Since the plant is native to the deep, rich, moist soils of open woodlands and the forest edge, it

Coreopsis lanceolata

does best in moist, well-drained soil high in organic matter. It grows tallest in deep soil and filtered shade, and ideally should not have more than four hours of direct sun each day. It will not flower well in deep shade, however.

Care Moderately easy. Water abundantly and fertilize regularly. The plant prefers cool soil, and it is best to mulch deeply throughout the summer. Division is an excellent means of increase but is rarely required for rejuvenation. Clumps can go for many years left alone.

Related species *Cimicifuga americana* is native to North America. Its foliage is more open and appears higher up the stalks. A smaller species, growing 2 to 4 feet tall, it blooms from August into September or October.

C. dahurica is native to Asia. Its foliage is bolder, and it never exceeds 4 or 5 feet in height. It blooms from August into fall.

C. foetida (sometimes listed as *C. simplex*) is more branched at the base, grows from 18 to 36 inches high, and

blooms in September and October.

Coreopsis lanceolata
(Ko-ree-*op*-sis)
Perennial coreopsis

Daisy family; native from Michigan south to Florida and New Mexico
Height: 2 feet
Spread: 1 foot
Hardy to zone 3

This perennial coreopsis produces bright golden yellow daisylike flowers on long stems above tufted, leafy mounds all summer long. They are most useful at the front or middle of the border.

The flowers have yellow "petals," actually ray flowers, with yellow or brown centers. They are about 3 inches wide and are produced generously in June through September.

The dark green leaves are long and straplike. The basal mounds support many flower stalks reaching 2 feet high.

Although it often reseeds, perennial coreopsis is seldom invasive like its annual cousins. It is long-lived, and the clumps expand slowly from

the center. Do not confuse this plant with several cultivars hybridized with *Coreopsis grandiflora*, as those are biennials.

How to start Easy to start from seed, and most cultivars will breed true to type. Sow outdoors in spring or summer up to two months prior to the first frost or, for flowers the first year, sow indoors six to eight weeks ahead of the last frost in spring. Keep the germinating medium at 60° to 70° F, and do not cover the seeds. It is also easy to start by division in spring.

Where to plant Coreopsis is extremely tolerant; give it any well-drained soil in full sun. Space plants 12 inches apart.

Care Easy. Water through dry periods, and feed occasionally. For longer bloom, remove faded flowers before they set seed. Leaf spot, rust, and powdery mildew can be severe problems. The foliage may also require protection from several chewing insects. Although clumps can go for many years before needing to be rejuvenated by division, it

is an excellent means of increase in early spring.

Related species *Coreopsis verticillata* (threadleaf coreopsis) is full, bushy, and grows to 3 feet tall. Its dense foliage is exceedingly fine in texture, misty, and soft in appearance. The plant is covered with small golden flowers all summer. Although not invasive, it performs best with frequent division. Of all the coreopsis, it is the most tolerant of dry soils. Threadleaf coreopsis is easy, restrained in growth, and long-lived.

C. grandiflora, a short-lived biennial and a weedy self-sower, blooms from mid-June through July.

Crambe cordifolia
(*Kram*-be)
Heartleaf crambe

Mustard family; native to the Caucasus
Height: 6 feet
Spread: 5 feet
Hardy to zone 6

There is no question that the large, bluish green heart-shaped leaves of heartleaf crambe create a statement.

Crambe cordifolia

Delphinium, Pacific Coast hybrids

Deeply lobed and thick, and covered with stiff hairs, each measures 2 or more feet across. The plant is described as "bold" by its admirers and as "coarse" by its detractors. In flower, though, there is no denying that it is spectacular. Its 6-foot flower stalk rises well above the foliage and bears literally thousands of tiny white flowers in clusters up to 4 feet across, looking like a gigantic baby's breath. The flowers appear from mid-June through July.

How to start Plant out divisions or nursery plants in spring or fall.

Where to plant Quite adaptable, but best in full sun in well-drained soil. For best results, the soil should be neutral to slightly alkaline. Because of its size, this plant is best in the background of a large perennial border.

Care Easy. Not subject to any particular problem. Although cabbage moths are attracted to its foliage, they rarely do much damage. Staking is not required.

Delphinium elatum
(Del-*fin*-ee-um)
Delphinium

Buttercup family; native from southern and central Europe to Siberia
Height: 4 to 8 feet
Spread: 1½ to 3 feet
Hardy to zone 2

Famous for their tall, bold spikes in rich blues, delphiniums are tricky to cultivate well. Although they grow beautifully in England, not many areas of the United States are as conducive to their growth. Grown well, they are unrivaled for dramatic effect.

The spurred flowers are mostly blue, but they also come in pink, white, red, violet, and purple. Individually, they are solid or often bicolored, with a contrasting white or black eye that is called a bee. Borne profusely along tall, vertical spikes, they bloom from June into July.

The dark green leaves are lobed and medium bold in texture. They are large and dense at the base, smaller and more scarce higher up. The stiffly erect stems appear in clumps

and are usually about 4 feet tall; under optimum conditions, however, they can reach 7 to 8 feet or more in height. Size also varies according to variety. The flowers are produced along the upper third or fourth of each stem, in dense vertical spikes.

Delphiniums are usually short-lived, often used as a biennial or a short-lived perennial. Under ideal conditions, the clumps expand gradually and the flower stalks increase in height and number as the years go by.

How to start The most successful method is to start container-grown plants purchased from a nursery in either early spring or early fall. Or start from divisions made in early spring, being sure to dust all cut surfaces with a fungicide. Avoid planting young starts or divisions too deeply. To start from seed, sow outdoors in spring or summer, or sow indoors, completely covered, at a temperature of 55° to 65° F.

Where to plant Soil must be rich, moist, well drained, and high in organic matter. It

should be slightly alkaline, or at least neutral. Provide full sun and good air circulation. Originally native to cool mountain meadows from Europe to Siberia, delphiniums decline rapidly in regions with hot, muggy summers. Space plants 18 to 36 inches apart.

Care Difficult, but worth the effort. Fertilize with a 5-10-10 fertilizer in early spring and again later in the growing season. Water abundantly, but never let the soil remain soggy. Try not to get the leaves wet. Staking is absolutely necessary to prevent the heavy spikes from breaking in the wind and to keep the plants from blowing or falling over. Because the roots are shallow and delicate, cultivate around them gently. As blooms fade, snip off the spike just below the lowest blossom. When the new growth from the base reaches 6 inches, cut the old stem clear to the ground. This will produce a second, though less spectacular, bloom in late summer.

Powdery mildew, crown rot, and several other fungal pests are problems, as are many insects, snails, and

Dianthus plumarius

Dicentra spectabilis

slugs. Applying both a fungicide and an insecticide at 10-day intervals is strongly advised. Remove and destroy all infected plants, and do not replant in the same area where crown rot has attacked. Protect the crowns from snails and slugs in fall and early spring. Mulch well after the ground freezes.

Delphiniums should be divided every third or fourth year. This is best done in early spring just as the new growth appears. Dust all cut surfaces with a fungicide.

Related species *Delphinium × belladonna* is a shorter species and may be longer-lived.

Dianthus plumarius
(Dy-*an*-thus)
Cottage pink, Scotch pink

Pink family; native to
central Europe
Height: 6 to 8 inches
Spread: 12 to 15 inches
Hardy to zone 3

Cottage pinks produce rose, pink, red, or white blossoms in spring on tufted, compact plants. Their gray-green leaves often persist through winter.

The flowers are about 1½ inches wide, fringed and lacy, and can be solid or bicolored, single or double. They appear in great quantities above the narrow, grasslike foliage, blooming in May and June.

The foliage forms dense mats 6 to 8 inches high, and the flower stems extend the height to a total of 12 inches. The mats expand gradually and indefinitely. Cottage pink will self-sow but is seldom invasive. Under favorable conditions, it is hardy and long-lived.

How to start Divisions or nursery plants are most frequently used. It is also easily grown from cuttings in the spring. The plant is easy to start from seed, but this will result in considerable variation.

Where to plant Needs well-drained soil, preferably on the alkaline side. It performs best in sandy soil amended with organic matter to retain moisture during the dry seasons. Give it full sun and good air circulation. Most cottage pinks are not for southern climates with hot, muggy summers; they do best

in cool coastal or mountainous areas of northern latitudes. Space plants 12 to 15 inches apart.

Care Moderately easy. Water during drought. Shear the flowers toward the end of the blooming season to encourage new growth and prevent reseeding. Leaf spot may become a problem in muggy weather or under crowded conditions; apply a fungicide as soon as it is detected. Division is best done in early spring and is one of the best means of increase. It also may be necessary every third or fourth year to prevent overcrowding.

Related species and varieties *Dianthus × allwoodii* is a hybrid strain generally agreed to be derived from crosses between the carnation and the cottage pink. The foliage is bolder and the plant stockier than *D. plumarius*, growing to about 12 inches tall. It is reportedly more tolerant of the hot, muggy summers of the Southeast than *D. plumarius*.

D. caryophyllus (carnation) includes types sold as an-

nuals, but although they are among the most tender of the species, they are true perennials. The hardiest border carnations will often survive temperatures as low as 12° F if protected by evergreen boughs. They are deliciously fragrant, much more so than greenhouse carnations.

D. deltoides (maiden pink) is a low-growing, mat-forming species with small, profuse flowers in June. The turflike foliage is semievergreen, often turning blackish and persisting throughout the winter.

Dicentra spectabilis
(Dy-*sen*-tra)
Bleeding-heart

Dutchman's breeches family; native to Japan
Height: 2½ feet
Spread: 3 feet
Hardy to zone 2

The flowers of the bleeding-heart are aptly named. They are puffy and suggest a heart with two drops of blood flaring up and out from the base, resulting in an overall lyre shape. The blossoms are purple, rose-pink with white tips, or all white.

Dicentra eximia

Dictamnus albus

They hang pendulously from horizontally arching and drooping stems. The flower stalks are up to 9 inches long, and are both among and above the foliage. Bleeding-heart blooms in the spring, usually in April and May.

The leaves are medium green, often with a slightly grayish cast, with deeply cut leaves that give the plant a finely textured appearance. The plant forms dense clumps of arching sprays of foliage 30 inches tall and up to 36 inches wide. Because of its relatively large size and its tendency to die down after blooming, bleeding-heart is best used as a specimen rather than massed. It is best grouped with other plants that will spread to cover up the bare place it leaves after blooming. It is a particularly good specimen plant in partial shade.

How to start Young plants purchased from a nursery are best planted in the spring before the new growth starts. Bleeding-heart can be started from seed, but this requires patience. Sow seed outdoors in late fall or early winter, or start indoors by sowing seed in small flats, freezing them for six weeks, and then germinating them at 55° to 60° F. Seedlings should appear in three to five weeks.

Where to plant Bleeding-heart prefers rich, moist, well-drained soil high in organic matter, and partial shade. It will tolerate full sun or deep shade quite well; however, in full sun the foliage will burn and die back quickly after flowering. It is also best to keep the plant out of drying winds. Space plants 2 feet apart.

Care Easy to moderately easy. Water abundantly and feed regularly, but cut back when the dormant period begins. Cultivars advertised as "blooming all summer" require assiduous deadheading. The chief problem with bleeding-heart is stem rot, which results from soggy soil and poor drainage. It is best not to disturb this plant; division is not necessary and is seldom successful.

Related species and varieties *Dicentra eximia* (fringed bleeding-heart) is notable for its beautiful gray-green, finely dissected foliage, which contrasts effectively with its deep rose to white flowers. It also has a longer bloom season. Several hybrid forms of this plant (probably crosses with *D. formosa*, among others) bloom intermittently all summer long if faded blossoms are removed regularly. One example is the hybrid 'Bountiful', with intense, deep red flowers off and on from June until frost.

D. formosa (western bleeding-heart) has flower stems about 1 foot tall and blossoms that are rose-purple to white in color. Under ideal conditions, it is an aggressive spreader.

Dictamnus albus
(Dik-*tam*-nus)
Gasplant

Citrus family; native from southern Europe to northern China
Height: 3 feet
Spread: 3 to 6 feet
Hardy to zone 2

The gasplant is a large, bushy perennial with showy flowers in early summer and excellent foliage useful for background. A lighted match held just below a blossom will ignite the minute amount of gas the flower releases with a soft pop. It doesn't hurt the flower at all. The flowers are white, pink, or purplish. Individually they are irregular and small, about 1 inch across, but are produced in great quantities in spikes at the top of the plant. They bloom in late May and June.

The foliage is dense, of medium texture, and remains attractive until frost. When the leaves are brushed or crushed, they exude the fragrance of lemons, to which the plant is related.

Gasplant grows to 3 feet high, and often spreads twice as wide. It is long-lived.

How to start Setting out young nursery plants is by far the most common method. This should be done in spring. To start from seed, sow outdoors where the plants are to grow in late fall or early winter. They will germinate the following spring. They are slow growing and take several years to become established. Seedlings do not take well to

Digitalis purpurea

Doronicum cordatum

transplanting, so it is better to start them in peat pots and plant them, peat pots and all.

Where to plant Gasplant prefers rich, well-drained soil high in organic matter. Avoid wet, soggy soils. Give it full sun or light shade. Allow 3 feet on all sides.

Care Easy. Gasplant responds to occasional feeding during the growing season. It has no serious pests. Division is never necessary and seldom successful. It resents transplanting and disturbance.

Related species and varieties *Dictamnus albus*, the species, has white flowers.

D. albus purpureus has pink or purple flowers.

Digitalis purpurea

(Dij-i-*tal*-is)
Foxglove

Snapdragon family; native to the western Mediterranean region
Height: 2 to 5 feet
Spread: 1½ to 2 feet
Hardy to zone 4

Although properly classified as a biennial, foxglove self-sows so generously, that, once planted, it can be considered a permanent fixture in the garden. The tall spikes of colorful flowers atop leafy stems lend an outstanding vertical effect, most valuable at the rear of the border. The plant is also excellent for informal, naturalistic plantings.

Flowers come in purple, pink, white, reddish, or yellow colors. Individually they are tubular, about 2½ inches long, and are ranged along one side of the stems. The flowers, which occur along the top 1 or 2 feet of the flower stalk, begin blooming at the bottom and stop at the top. They appear in June and July.

The leaves are large, somewhat rough and wrinkled, and dark green on the upper surface and light green beneath, where they are covered with whitish hairs. They are dense at the base of the plant, becoming smaller and more scarce toward the top.

Foxglove will sometimes bloom a second time with smaller spikes if the flowers are removed before they can set seed. The plant self-sows abundantly where conditions are favorable. The foliage tends to look ratty once the plant is past bloom.

How to start Plant nursery plants in spring, or sow seed outdoors in late spring or early summer, or indoors at a constant temperature of 70° F. Do not cover the seeds. Germination occurs in one to three weeks.

Where to plant Foxglove does well in acid, moist, well-drained soil high in organic matter. The plant is partial to deep shade but tolerates full sun. Hybrid varieties are usually less particular about soil. Space plants 18 to 24 inches apart.

Care Moderately easy. Removing flower spikes before they set seed encourages second-year bloom, but it will be inferior. Otherwise allow the plants to self-sow, and remove plants after they have seeded. Fungicides protect against powdery mildew and leaf spot. Insecticides protect against aphids, mealybugs, and Japanese beetles.

Division is not applicable, as the plants usually die after they flower.

Related species and varieties The Excelsior hybrids are choice because they produce flowers on all sides of the stem. The flowers are so tightly packed that they do not droop but are held at right angles to the stem. They come in pastel shades of pink, white, yellow, and rose. Seeds usually come in mixed colors, as do nursery seedlings.

Some species of foxglove are truly perennial, but they have fewer and less colorful flowers.

Doronicum cordatum

(Do-*ron*-i-cum)
Leopard's-bane

Daisy family; native to southeastern Europe and western Asia
Height: 8 to 12 inches
Spread: 12 to 24 inches
Hardy to zone 4

The spring-blooming, daisylike, bright yellow flowers of leopard's-bane appear in

Echinacea purpurea

Echinops exaltatus

great quantities above clusters of large, heart-shaped leaves.

Each blossom is 2 to 3 inches across and appears on its own 9- to 15-inch stem. The plant blooms in May, and the foliage often dies down after blooming is complete.

The foliage is medium to bold in texture and is produced in low basal clumps of 3- to 5-inch leaves. The clumps grow 8 to 12 inches high and, with flowers, the plant often reaches 1 to 2 feet in height.

Leopard's-bane produces shallow, dense, fibrous roots. The clumps expand rapidly and start dying out in the center unless divided. Since the foliage dies out early in the season, the plant is best used as a specimen rather than massed, and should be combined with other plants that will spread to cover the empty space. In warm climates with long, mild autumns, the foliage may come back, and the plant bloom a second time.

How to start Purchase nursery plants or take divisions in August while the plant is dormant. Or sow seed outdoors in late spring or summer. Germination is slow and erratic but usually occurs within four weeks.

Where to plant Needs rich, moist soil high in organic matter. It prefers partial shade, especially in hot climates. Space 12 to 15 inches apart.

Care Easy. Water moderately during the growing season. There are no serious pests. Division for rejuvenation is usually required every two to four years and is best done during dormancy in August or very early spring. It is an excellent means of increase.

Echinacea purpurea
(Ek-in-*ay*-see-uh)
Purple coneflower

Daisy family; native from Ohio to Iowa, south to Louisiana and Georgia
Height: 3 to 5 feet
Spread: 2 to 5 feet
Hardy to zone 3

The purple coneflower is a large, bold plant with daisylike flowers that have large, drooping "petals."

Named varieties are much superior to the species.

The flowers come in purple and, occasionally, white varieties. The "petals," technically ray flowers, droop back toward the stem. The eye is conical, bristly, and dark. The flowers are 3 to 4 inches wide and appear at the ends of many long, branched stems. They bloom from July to September.

The foliage is boldly textured leaves that are dense at the base of the plant, smaller and more scattered toward the top. The plant forms a clump of many stems, which are branched, semierect, and spreading.

Purple coneflower is long-lived and not invasive.

How to start Take divisions or purchase plants from a nursery. Seeds do not produce plants true to type.

Where to plant Soil should be sandy and well drained. Provide full sun or light shade; the latter produces richer colors. The plant is native to North American prairies and meadows, mostly at the edges of woods. It is drought and wind tolerant. Space plants 18 to 24 inches apart.

Care Moderately easy. It responds to light feeding and moderate watering. Never allow the soil to remain soggy. Japanese beetles can ruin this plant very quickly; protect it with traps, an insecticide, or assiduous handpicking. Clumps require division every third or fourth year for rejuvenation. This is also an excellent means of increase and should be performed in early spring just as new growth appears.

Varieties It is best to purchase named varieties; they tend to have bigger flowers and better color than the species.

'The King' is probably the most famous hybrid. Its 6-inch flowers are a brilliant reddish purple with brown centers. It grows to 3 feet and has a refined appearance.

'White Lustre' has creamy white flowers that are produced in tremendous profusion, even in severe drought. (Its foliage and structure are quite bold.)

Echinops exaltatus

Euphorbia epithymoides

Echinops exaltatus

(*Ek*-in-ops)
Globe thistle

Daisy family; native to Russia
Height: 3 to 4 feet
Spread: 1½ to 2 feet
Hardy to zone 3

Globe thistles are large, dramatic plants with round flower heads and spiny, toothed leaves.

The flowers, which bloom from July through August, are various shades of blue. Individually tiny, they are gathered into dense, bristly balls about 2 inches across. These balls occur singly at the ends of branched stems. They are impressive in the garden, and dry well for winter flower arrangements if picked and hung to dry before they are fully open.

The leaves are deeply toothed and are deep green on the top and white on the bottom. The plant produces dense clumps of semierect, spreading stems that expand gradually and require periodic thinning. The roots are dense and about 1 foot deep, making the plant difficult to divide. It tends to get leggy.

How to start Divisions or young container plants from a nursery are best. Be sure to acquire named varieties, since seedlings are extremely variable and usually inferior. Plant in early spring.

Where to plant Prefers well-drained soil of only average fertility. Rich soil will produce taller, more open plants. Full sun is best, but the plant tolerates partial shade. It withstands considerable drought but responds to adequate moisture. It is absolutely intolerant of soggy soil. Space plants 18 to 24 inches apart.

Care Moderately easy. Globe thistle requires little special attention and has no serious pests. Although difficult due to the deep and extensive root system, division is necessary every third or fourth year. It is an excellent means of increase and is best done in early spring.

Varieties The best cultivar is 'Taplow Blue', which has steel blue, 3-inch flower heads.

Euphorbia epithymoides

(formerly *E. polychroma*)
(Yew-*for*-bee-a)
Cushion spurge

Spurge family; native to eastern Europe
Height: 12 to 24 inches
Spread: 12 to 15 inches
Hardy to zone 4

The bright yellow-green floral bracts in spring; an excellent, neat, mounded habit; and clean foliage all summer long make this plant attractive as a specimen or at the front of the border. It flowers from late April to early June.

The dark green leaves turn a rich, dark red in fall. Of medium texture, the foliage is pest free and attractive all season. The plant forms a dense mound.

Cushion spurge is more restrained in growth and less invasive than some other spurges; however, it does self-sow. It is long-lived.

How to start Set out young nursery plants in early spring. It is also easy to start from seed sown outdoors in late fall or early spring.

Where to plant The plant tolerates nearly any soil but can spread invasively if the soil is rich and moist. It will take dry, poor soils and remain in excellent condition. Give it full sun. The neat, symmetrical habit is best as a specimen, but if planted in groups, space them 12 to 15 inches apart.

Care Easy. Spurges are remarkably tolerant of drought, heat, and neglect. There are no serious pests. They resent disturbance and do not transplant well. In rich, moist soil, careful division in either spring or fall may be necessary to check excessive spreading.

Related species *Euphorbia corollata* (flowering spurge) is quite unlike cushion spurge. It produces misty sprays of tiny white flowers, resembling baby's breath, in July and August, and the foliage turns a deep red in fall. It self-sows plentifully, is extremely tough and adaptable, and never needs staking.

E. cyparissias (Cyprus spurge) is low, bushy, and mat forming. It has narrow, linear

Filipendula rubra

Gaillardia × grandiflora

leaves of fine texture, and yellow-green floral bracts in May and June. It is best planted in dry, poor soil as it becomes a rampant weed in good soil.

E. myrsinites (myrtle euphorbia) is evergreen and very hardy. It grows 3 to 6 inches high and over a foot wide. Though invasive, it is a good ground cover in dry, poor soil. It is the best spurge for the Deep South.

Filipendula rubra
(Fil-i-*pen*-dew-la)
Queen-of-the-prairie

Rose family; native from Pennsylvania to Iowa, and south to Georgia and Kentucky
Height: 4 to 6 feet
Spread: 1 to 2 feet
Hardy to zone 3

This is a tall, stately plant with large, feathery pink plumes in midsummer and lush foliage that remains attractive all season. It is a fine choice for the rear of the border. Flowers appear in late June and last through July.

The medium-green, compound leaves are dense and

lush. The plant produces leafy stems 4 to 6 feet high, each bearing flowers at the top. It is restrained in growth, never invasive, and long-lived.

How to start   Purchase nursery plants or make divisions in spring. If started from seed, the seed must be fresh and should be sown outdoors in early fall.

Where to plant   Since its native habitat is the moist, deep soil of bottomland prairies and meadows, plant queen-of-the-prairie in fertile, moist soil high in organic matter. It flowers best in full sun but is quite tolerant of partial shade. Space 12 to 24 inches apart.

Care   Moderately easy. Water abundantly and feed regularly. During wet or humid weather mildew may present a problem. Control with a fungicide. Although the plant seldom requires division for rejuvenation, it is an excellent means of increase. Divide in early spring just as the new growth begins.

Related species and varieties   *Filipendula vulgaris* (dropwort) grows to only 2

feet. Misty clusters of ivory flowers, single or double, appear in June above finely textured, ferny foliage. It withstands drought and poor soil and is the best choice for the Southeast. The double 'Flore Pleno' flowers longer than the species.

F. rubra venusta (Martha Washington plume) is superior to the species, with huge, 12-inch, pink plumes. It blooms in July and early August.

F. ulmaria (queen-of-the-meadow) is similar to *F. rubra*, except that the flowers are white. Growing to 4 feet, it blooms from June to mid-July.

Gaillardia × grandiflora
(Gay-*lar*-dee-a)
Blanket-flower

Daisy family; of hybrid origin, parents native to the mountainous West and the Southeast in the United States
Height: 1½ to 3 feet
Spread: 1 to 1½ feet
Hardy to zone 2

The blanket-flower is a relatively short-lived perennial

with bright red, bronze, or yellow flowers, often in combination. Best planted in the front of the border in groups of three or more, it provides bloom all summer long.

The daisylike flowers have outer rays that can be solid or bicolored, and a central eye that can be yellow, brown, or purple. They are 3 to 4 inches across and appear in great quantities from June to September.

The foliage is dark green, dense, and of medium texture, with hairy, lance-shaped leaves. Blanket-flower forms clumps of multibranched, erect to spreading stems and can grow to 3 feet tall. The plant spreads outward by underground rhizomes.

How to start   Easiest by nursery plants or divisions made in early spring. Named varieties purchased as young plants from a nursery are usually root cuttings. Plants often do not come true from seed, but to start by seed, sow outdoors in early spring or summer for flowering plants the next season. Or sow indoors in late winter at a constant 70° F.

Geranium sanguineum

Geum hybrid

Do not cover, as the seeds require light to germinate.

Where to plant The soil must be very well drained and of average to poor fertility. Rich, moist soils lead to an open, sprawling habit and an early death. Give it full sun. It tolerates heat and drought well. Space plants 10 to 15 inches apart.

Care Do not overwater or overfertilize. To prolong the bloom period, remove spent flowers before they set seed.

Taller plants may require staking. A regular program of using both an insecticide and a fungicide will help prevent leaf spot, powdery mildew, aster yellows, and damage from various sucking insects. Carefully remove and destroy any plant infected with aster yellows.

Blanket-flower requires annual division to perpetuate blooming from year to year. During the summer, prune roots by inserting a spade in a circle 6 inches around the crown. This stimulates the production of new plants from the severed roots. Transplant these in early spring.

Geranium sanguineum

(Jer-*ay*-nee-um)
Bloodred geranium

Geranium family; native to Europe and Asia
Height: 1½ feet
Spread: 2 feet
Hardy to zone 3

The bloodred geranium (named for its fall foliage color) is a hardy herbaceous perennial with deeply cut leaves; a mounded, spreading form; and small, single magenta flowers. It should not be confused with *Pelargonium*, which is often called geranium in nurseries.

Flower varieties come in purplish pink, red, or white. The blossoms are from 1 to 2 inches wide, have five petals, and appear on 8-inch stems. They bloom from May to August.

The dense, bright green leaves turn bright red in the fall. It is long-lived and may spread and self-sow invasively.

How to start Sow fresh seed outdoors in early spring, or indoors at a constant 70° F. Germination should occur in one to five weeks. It can also

be started either from divisions made in spring or stem cuttings made in summer.

Where to plant Geraniums adapt to most soils except very wet or very dry ones, and do best with good drainage. Give them full sun or partial shade. Soils of only average fertility are best, as rich, moist soils promote invasive growth. Space plants 12 inches apart.

Care Moderately easy. Do not overfertilize. The plant is little disturbed by pests. Bloodred geranium will require rejuvenation by division every three or four years. This is also an excellent means of increase and should be done in spring.

Related species and varieties *Geranium endressii* grows 15 to 18 inches high and is best known for its varieties 'Johnson's Blue', with light gentian blue flowers, and 'Wargrave Pink', with clear pink flowers. Both plants will flower over a long season, nearly all summer, if cut back after the first wave of blooms in May.

G. himalayense (lilac cranesbill), formerly *G.*

grandiflorum, has blue, purple, or lavender flowers during May and July on 2-foot, mounded, spreading plants.

G. sanguineum var. *prostratum* (often called *G. lancastrense*) is more restrained and neat in growth habit than the species, seldom taller than 6 or 8 inches, with bright rose-pink blossoms nearly all summer long.

Geum hybrids

(*Jee*-um)
Geum, avens

Rose family; the various parents are native to the colder temperate regions in both the Northern and Southern hemispheres
Height: 1 to 2 feet
Spread: 1 to 1½ feet
Hardy to zone 5

The many hybrid varieties of geum produce long, branching stems bearing flowers in bright reds, oranges, and yellows, often in electric hues. They are attractive both as specimens and in the mixed border.

The flowers are small, up to about 1 inch across, and

Arrhenatherum elatius var. *bulbosum* 'Variegatum'

Calamagrostis epigeous

single, with double and semi-double varieties. They appear in great profusion from May to August and even longer if spent flowers are removed before they can set seed.

The stems and flowers radiate in all directions from dense basal clumps of large, deep green leaves. Irregular and toothed, the leaves also appear on the 24- to 30-inch stems, becoming smaller and fewer as they ascend. The stems are branched and open.

Although all geums grow slowly, the newer hybrids are even slower to increase; however, they are also longer lived. The plants are never invasive.

How to start   The best results come with named varieties from nursery plants or divisions made in late summer. Divisions usually bloom the next spring. Geums are easily started from seed sown outdoors in spring or summer, but the hybrids will not breed true. Few seeds will germinate, so sow thickly.

Where to plant   Geum is quite choosy about location.

The soil must have excellent drainage and sufficient organic matter. Water abundantly during the growing season. Wet soil in winter is fatal. Give them full sun. They are reliably hardy if the soil is dry, and they perform best in regions of cool summers. Space plants 12 to 18 inches apart.

Care   Moderately difficult unless planted correctly; otherwise, they need little attention. Remove spent flowers to keep plants neat and extend bloom into fall. Geum has no serious pests. Division is an excellent means of increase and is best done in late summer. The older varieties will require division every other year, but the newer hybrids can often go for many years before needing rejuvenation.

Grasses, Ornamental

Arrhenatherum elatius var. *bulbosum* 'Variegatum'
Variegated bulbous oat grass
Hardy to zone 5

This grass is loosely tufted and deciduous, with attractive,

striped leaves that have a clean white margin. When in flower (June to September), the plants may reach 3 feet in height and spread. This cultivar may be invasive, especially in rich soils. It is easy to grow in rich soil and either full sun or partial shade. In hot weather the foliage may brown and turn unsightly; it is often recommended that this grass be cut back once about midsummer. Divide every two to three years to maintain vigor. It is native to Europe and western Asia.

Calamagrostis epigeous 'Hortorum'
(also listed as *Calamagrostis* × *acutiflora* 'Stricta')
Reed grass
Hardy to zone 5

This cultivar of reed grass is considered indispensable by many advanced gardeners for its narrowly vertical habit from 3 to 6 feet tall. Rich, foxy, golden-red flower spikes that are attractive all winter long begin blooming in late June and July, earlier than most grasses. It is easy to grow

in any fertile soil and full sun, as long as it is kept moist. Reed grass is one of the few grasses that will thrive in wet clay soil; it actually prefers boggy situations. Reed grass is native discontinuously from northern Europe to eastern and southern Africa.

Cortaderia selloana
Pampas grass
Perennial only in mild climates (zone 7 and south)

This large, coarse grass is huge, from 4 to 20 feet high. It is upright and spreading to mounded in form, with huge, fluffy plumes up to 3 feet long atop stems that may reach 20 feet. The flowers can be creamy, buff, or pale pink, and they appear in the fall (summer in the mildest climates). Pampas grass performs quite well in dry, poor soils, but fertile, moist ones are best. It prefers full sun. Occasionally dwarf or pink selections are offered. A new selection with yellow variegated leaves, 'Gold Band', is available.

Cortaderia jubata is another species occasionally

Cortaderia selloana

Elymus arenarius

Deschampsia caespitosa

Festuca ovina var. 'Glauca'

encountered in nurseries, usually mistakenly identified as *C. selloana*. *C. jubata* self-sows profusely and is well on its way to becoming a noxious pest, especially in the milder climates of the West Coast. Unfortunately, it is extremely difficult to differentiate from pampas grass, especially when immature.

Deschampsia caespitosa
Tufted hair grass

Hardy to zone 5

Forming a 3-foot, finely textured, tufted mound, this hair grass is useful in either sun or shade, in moist soil or dry. The leaves are evergreen and effective all winter long. Feathery, whitish green flowers are produced from late June through August, which is early for most grasses.

Elymus arenarius
Blue lyme grass

Hardy to zone 4

Silvery blue foliage is the distinctive feature of this coarse, invasive grass. Unless it is restrained, the persistent, creeping rhizomes can become quite a nuisance. It grows 2 to

4 feet tall, and the leaves tend to grow in every direction, creating a jumbled, coarse appearance. Blue lyme grass will grow in nearly any soil, but it is intolerant of shade.

Festuca ovina var. 'Glauca'
Dwarf blue fescue

Hardy to zone 4

This is a popular, small, tufted grass with finely textured, silvery blue evergreen foliage. It grows from 6 to 12 inches high in a neat mound. It must have well-drained soil and prefers full sun or light shade. Frequent division is required, as the center of the clump tends to die out, especially in moist, rich soil. Removing the flowers as they appear tends to prolong its useful life. In southern California, dwarf blue fescue is one of the few gray plants that will do well with light shade. Its color is better without the browning at the tips sometimes caused by the sun.

Hakonechloa macra 'Aureo-variegata'

Hardy to at least zone 4

This grass is a relatively recent introduction to U. S.

horticulture from the mountains and forests of Japan. The long, deciduous, arching leaves are variegated creamy yellow. The plant spreads slowly by rhizomes and is never invasive. Equally effective in pots or planted in large drifts, the plant presents a neat, uniform appearance, reaching up to 12 inches high. Grow this grass in acid (pH 5.5 to 6.0) soil that has both excellent drainage and plenty of organic matter. Bright, indirect light is best. Full sun is not recommended.

Helictotrichon sempervirens
(formerly *Avena sempervirens*)
Blue oat grass

Hardy to zone 5

Resembling a large blue fescue, this tufted, mounded grass with bluish green leaves reaches 2 to 3 feet high. The leaves are of fine texture. Plant it in any soil in full sun. In humid environments it is prone to fungal attack. The foliage browns in winter.

Miscanthus sinensis
Eulalia grass

Hardy to zone 4

Large, striking, upright, and gracefully arching at the top, eulalia grass forms dense clumps 6 to 12 feet tall. The foliage is medium-fine in texture, turning a rich gold that is effective through the winter. The flowers, with their pinkish or silvery 7- to 10-inch plumes, are also attractive from fall into winter. The plant will perform well in any soil, and should have full sun.

'Gracillimus' is a finely textured cultivar with narrow, somewhat curly leaves. 'Variegatus' and 'Zebrinus' have foliage and stems in combinations of green with yellow or white. These cultivars are smaller than the species, rarely exceeding 6 or 7 feet in height.

Molinia caerulea 'Variegata'
Purple moor grass

Hardy to zone 5

This is a densely tufted, deciduous grass. The leaves are medium to fine in texture and longitudinally striped with creamy white. The flowers are purplish pink, up to 16 inches long, and appear in late summer and early fall. The

Pennisetum alopecuroides

Schizachyrium scoparium

Molinia caerulea 'Variegata'

plant ranges from 18 to 24 inches high and wide. This grass prefers acid to neutral soil and full sun. It dislikes alkaline soil. It is native to open moorlands and heaths of Europe and southwestern and northern Asia.

Pennisetum alopecuroides
Fountain grass

Hardy to zone 5

One of the most graceful and popular of ornamental perennial grasses, fountain grass grows in a loose tuft 2 to 3½ feet high. From late August through October, coppery tan flowers arch out like water spraying out of a fountain. In late fall the foliage turns yellow. Give it full sun, fertile soil, and enough room to develop its 3- to 4-foot mature diameter. It is native to the steppes of Asia.

Schizachyrium scoparium
(sometimes listed as *Andropogon scoparius*)

Little bluestem

Hardy to zone 4

This native of the eastern United States is useful either for naturalizing or in the border. Growing from 1½ to 4 feet tall, it presents a stiffly upright form with finely textured, bluish green leaves that turn bronze or reddish and remain attractive all winter. The fluffy, small white flowers and seeds are effective from July into winter. It will grow in nearly any soil but prefers those that are well drained and dry. Give it full sun. A striking blue selection is available from Nebraska.

Gypsophila paniculata
(Jip-*soff*-ill-a)

Baby's breath

Pink family; native from central and eastern Europe to central Africa
Height: 3 feet
Spread: 3 to 4 feet
Hardy to zone 3

The cloudlike mists of tiny white or pink flowers of baby's breath are a familiar sight in the perennial garden. Use it as a complement to bold-textured plants or as a focal point in the border.

The flowers are usually white, but some varieties are pink or have a pinkish cast. The individual blossoms are tiny, either single or double, and are produced in massive quantities on slender, multibranched stems. The effect is airy and delicate. Baby's breath blooms in July, but shearing spent flowers will prolong it into September.

The smooth, grayish green leaves are rarely noticeable below the drifts of flowers. The many stems are covered to the ground with blossoms, making the overall shape rounded and fluffy. Baby's breath reaches 3 feet high and as wide or even wider. The plant is long-lived in a favorable location and is never invasive. It forms thick, dense, fleshy roots.

How to start Easily started from seed sown outdoors in spring or early summer, if the species is desired. Or sow indoors in spring at 60° to 70° F. Named cultivars, often superior, are generally grafted onto the species rootstock. These should be purchased and planted in early spring. Be sure to set the grafted varieties with the graft union 1 inch below the soil level.

Where to plant The soil must be well drained and alkaline and preferably low in fertility. Soggy soil, especially in winter, is usually fatal. Rock garden conditions are ideal. Give it full sun. Space plants 24 to 30 inches apart.

Care Moderately easy. The plant is difficult to stake, and large varieties and vigorous plants will need support to keep them from flopping and spreading open. The best method is to place a wire basket about 15 to 18 inches high and wide over young plants for the stems to grow through. In acid soils apply lime yearly, but do not let it come into direct contact with the fleshy roots. To prolong bloom, keep flowers sheared before they set seed. Once established, it needs little attention.

Although the plant is usually free of pests and disease, leafhoppers and aster yellows have been reported. North of zone 6, mulching over the winter to protect from cold is advised; however, do not cover the crown until after the ground is completely frozen, or it is likely to rot.

Gypsophila paniculata

Helenium autumnale

The thick roots are difficult to divide, and plants resent transplanting. Division is discouraged, but is best done in spring.

Related species and varieties 'Bristol Fairy' is the most common cultivar, with excellent double white flowers on 4-foot plants.

'Pink Fairy' is a small, restrained plant growing only 18 inches high. It has a long bloom season, producing pink double flowers from July to frost.

Gypsophila repens (creeping baby's breath) is a low-growing species from 6 to 18 inches high that spreads widely by creeping, rooting stems. It is good in the front of the border, in the rock garden, or trailing down walls. One of the most popular varieties is a pink form, 'Rosy Veil'.

Helenium autumnale

(Hel-*ee*-nee-um)
Sneezeweed

Daisy family; native to most of continental North America
Height: 2½ to 6 feet
Spread: 1½ to 2 feet
Hardy to zone 3

Sneezeweed is an unfortunate name for this plant, as it neither causes sneezing nor is a weed. The small, daisylike flowers, despite their massive quantity, present a delicate appearance in the garden, as the rays of each flower head point gracefully back toward the stem. It is a relative of the sunflower and the black-eyed-susan.

Flowers occur in shades of red, orange, or yellow, with solid or bicolored "petals," or rays. The flowers are 1 or 2 inches across and appear at the ends of branched stems. They bloom in late July through frost.

The medium to dark green leaves are linear, up to 6 inches long, and larger and more numerous at the base of the plant. The stems are erect and then arch and spread at the top, making the plant wider at the top than at the base. Sneezeweed can grow from 30 inches to 6 feet tall, depending upon the variety and growing conditions.

These are vigorous plants and rapidly become crowded if not divided regularly. Grown properly, they are long-lived and seldom invasive.

How to start The cultivars, which are usually hybrid, will not breed true from seed. The species can be sown indoors in early spring at 60° F and will germinate in one week. Purchased plants are usually grown from stem cuttings or divisions and are best planted in early spring.

Where to plant Best in soil of only average fertility that is high in moisture and organic matter. Sneezeweed is tolerant of many poor soils, however, including heavy, wet clay. Give it full sun. Space plants 18 to 24 inches apart.

Care Moderately easy. The taller varieties need staking. Pinch growing tips regularly until mid-June to promote heavier flowering and bushy, dense growth. Sneezeweed has few serious problems, although rust and leaf spot have been reported. Divide the plant every other year to prevent overcrowding. Vigorous plants may need annual division, but slower-growing hybrids may go as long as four years without it.

Helianthus decapetalus var. multiflorus

(Hee-li-*an*-thus)
Thinleaf sunflower

Daisy family; native from Maine to Georgia and west to Illinois and Minnesota
Height: 4 to 5 feet
Spread: 1½ to 2 feet
Hardy to zone 3

This large, bushy sunflower produces great quantities of yellow or gold flowers in late summer. The blooms resemble dahlias and are excellent in the border and for cut flowers.

The blossoms may be either single or double and are 3 to 4 inches in diameter. They appear in clusters at the ends of branched stems, blooming from August until frost.

Unlike many other sunflowers, the foliage of the thinleaf sunflower usually stays attractive all season long. The large, oval leaves are a dark, dull green. The leafy stems are erect and somewhat spreading toward the top, where they become increasingly branched. Most varieties reach 4 to 5 feet high.

Helianthus decapetalus

Heliopsis helianthoides scabra

The plant forms swollen, fleshy roots similar to tubers. It is long-lived, restrained in growth, and never invasive.

How to start It is best to purchase named cultivars from a nursery or to divide selected plants in spring, because seed produces many inferior plants.

Where to plant These sunflowers are native to moist woods and bottom meadows and so prefer moist, well-drained soil high in organic matter. Although full sun is best, partial shade is tolerated well. Good air circulation is a distinct advantage. Space plants 18 to 24 inches apart.

Care Easy. The tallest varieties may require staking. Water adequately and feed occasionally. It has few serious pests, although mildew can be a problem in moist locations with poor air circulation. Protect plants with a fungicide. Division is the best means of increase but is seldom needed for rejuvenation. Divide in early spring.

Heliopsis helianthoides scabra
(He-li-*op*-thus)
Oxeye, false-sunflower

Daisy family; native to eastern North America
Height: 3 to 4 feet
Spread: 2 feet
Hardy to zone 3

The yellow or gold flowers of oxeye are produced in fabulous abundance over a long season. For its bright, solid color and length of bloom, it is nearly indispensable in the perennial border.

The flowers may be single or semidouble, but most cultivars are fully double. Resembling zinnias, they are 3 to 4 inches across and appear at the ends of long, branched, leafy stems. They bloom from early July to frost.

The dark green leaves are lush, dense, and lance shaped or oblong to 5 inches in length. The plant is erect to spreading, bushy, and widest at the top. Always restrained in growth and never invasive, it is long-lived when divided periodically.

How to start Divide named cultivars in fall or spring, or

purchase nursery plants. Plants may vary considerably when started from seed.

Where to plant Best in moist, well-drained soil of average to moderately high fertility and high in organic matter. Give it full sun. Space plants 24 inches apart.

Care Moderately easy. Water abundantly, especially during drought. Fertilize regularly. Aphids are the chief pest problem, especially on plants grown in poor soil. Otherwise, there are no serious pests. Rejuvenate by dividing every three or four years. Division is also the best means of increase.

Helleborus niger
(Hell-e-*bor*-us)
Christmas-rose

Buttercup family; native to Europe
Height: 1 to 1½ feet
Spread: 1 to 2 feet
Hardy to zone 3

Not even remotely related to roses, this is an evergreen perennial that blooms in winter with large white flowers, often flushed with pale pink.

It is useful in shady woodland spots under the canopy of deciduous trees.

The flowers are produced at the ends of several clustered stems. They have five showy sepals, 2 to 4 inches across, surrounding a center of attractive yellow stamens. They can bloom as early as November or as late as March or April, although the latter is more common. Winter bloom depends upon warm spells that thaw the soil.

The foliage appears to grow directly out of the soil without stems. The large, smooth, deep green leaves are compound, divided into seven or more leaflets, and are evergreen in zone 6 and south.

The clumps of foliage expand slowly by rhizomatous roots. The plant is long-lived, restrained in growth, and never invasive.

How to start Best started from nursery plants or divisions planted in spring. It can be started from seed, but considerable time will elapse before the plants are large enough to transplant. Young

Helleborus niger

Hemerocallis 'Northbrook Star'

(first-year) self-sown seedlings collected from around established plants are easy to transplant.

Where to plant Needs well-drained, moist soil high in organic matter and preferably acid or neutral (pH 6.5 to 7.0). The plant requires shade in summer and partial sun in winter, such as is found under the boughs of deciduous trees or shrubs (but try to avoid competing, greedy roots).

Care Moderately difficult; the plant is choosy about location. Keep it evenly moist, and never allow it to dry out. Mulch well with organic matter in summer and irrigate regularly, especially during drought. If the soil is extremely acid, apply lime yearly, but avoid letting it contact the roots, which are sensitive. Fertilize rarely, if ever, as the roots are easily damaged by nitrogen. Leaf spot is occasionally troublesome but easy to treat with a fungicide.

Christmas-rose resents disturbance of any kind and never needs division for rejuvenation. Dividing for increase is possible but difficult and should be performed in early spring after blooming is complete. Carefully separate the roots, ensuring that each portion has several roots and "eyes" (developing leaf buds). Set the roots so that the eyes are about an inch below soil level.

Related species and varieties *Helleborus lividus corsicus* (Corsican hellebore) has apple green blossoms in large clusters in early spring. This is the best *Helleborus* for the mild-climate regions of the Southwest. Although reportedly hardy to zone 6, in the northern limits of its range it should be well protected from cold, drying winds in the winter.

H. orientalis (lenten-rose) blooms from March into May. Varieties are available with flowers in colors from chocolate and purplish green to pink and white. The foliage is a lighter green than the Christmas-rose, but the structure and cultural needs are nearly the same. It is hardy to zone 5 and is reported to be the best *Helleborus* for the Southeast.

Hemerocallis hybrids

(Hem-er-o-*kall*-is)
Daylily

Lily family; most hybrids have parents native to Japan
Height: 3 to 4 feet
Spread: 1½ to 3 feet
Hardy to zone 3

Daylilies are very easy, long-lasting perennials with attractive foliage and showy flowers. The individual blossoms last only a day but are continually produced over a long season.

Daylilies come in many colors, with flowers in shades of cream, yellow, orange, red, pink, and violet, often striped and bicolored. Individually they are from 3 to 5 inches long and open just as wide. They appear at the ends of long stems. Some varieties are deliciously fragrant.

Flowering generally lasts three to four weeks, but this varies according to the cultivar. The bloom season is commonly divided into early (late May and June), middle (July), and late (August into September), although considerable overlapping occurs.

The bright green, handsome, straplike leaves grow 1 to 2 feet long and are effective all season. The leaves arch out from the base of the plant, forming a mound of foliage. Stems and flowers arise from this mound.

Depending upon variety, daylilies can reach from 20 inches to 3 or 4 feet tall, including flowers. They all form a tough, heavy, tuberous root system. Some varieties are evergreen in mild climates (zone 8 and south).

Daylilies are exceedingly long-lived, and the clumps expand indefinitely. They are restrained in growth, permanent, not invasive, and compete well with roots of trees and shrubs. Hybrids do not reseed.

How to start Best from nursery stock or division in spring or late summer. Sowing seed is a complex and intriguing undertaking for those gardeners interested in selecting and breeding.

Where to plant Daylilies are highly adaptable but perform best in well-drained soil high in organic matter and of

Hemerocallis 'Finest Hour'

Heuchera sanguinea

only average fertility. Tolerating shade or sun well, they seem to prefer full sun in northern areas and partial shade in the hot South. However, delicate colors tend to fade quickly in full sun. Too rich a soil leads to the rapid growth of lush foliage and few flowers. Space plants 18 to 36 inches apart.

Care   Very easy. Water through dry periods and give an occasional light feeding. To improve appearance, remove the flower stalks after their blossoms are spent. The plant has no serious pests. Although most varieties can be left alone permanently, some of the more vigorous ones give improved performance with division every six or seven years. Division of mature plants is an arduous task due to the heavy root system, but it is still the best means of increase. Divide in spring or late summer.

Varieties   Cultivars are too numerous to mention here. Extensive breeding has resulted in thousands.

Heuchera sanguinea
(*Hew*-kair-a)
Coralbells

Saxifrage family; native to New Mexico and Arizona south to Mexico
Height: 1 to 2 feet
Spread: 1 to 1½ feet
Hardy to zone 3

Airy clusters of tiny, bell-shaped flowers top the long, delicate flower stalks of coralbells. They are effective in the front of borders or as a small-scale ground cover in either sun or partial shade and are hardy far north of their natural range.

The flowers are pink, red, white, or chartreuse. They bloom in June and July, but flowering can be prolonged into September by the removal of faded flower stalks.

The attractive basal clumps of foliage are evergreen. The leaves are dark or bright green, rounded, and 2 to 4 inches across. Some varieties are marbled with bronze or silver and take on a reddish cast in fall that lasts through the winter. The plant grows 10 to 24 inches high.

The clumps of foliage will expand gradually from the center by the growth of long, fleshy surface roots. Although coralbells produces great quantities of seed, some of which may germinate in the garden, it could never be considered invasive. It is long-lived.

How to start   Nursery plants or division in spring are the most common methods of starting. Make sure that each thick stem has a few roots, and plant the crowns 1 inch below the soil level. Coralbells is also easy to start from leaf cuttings made in late fall. Each cutting needs a short section of leaf stalk, in addition to an entire leaf, to root in sand. Seed sown outdoors in early spring will produce flowering plants the next year. Merely press the seed into the soil and do not cover, as it needs light to germinate. Or sow indoors in late winter or early spring at 50° to 60° F. Germination takes about 20 days. Hybrid seed does not breed true.

Where to plant   Coralbells is very adaptable but performs best in well-drained soils rich in organic matter. It prefers full sun but does quite well in partial shade. Space plants 9 to 15 inches apart.

Care   Easy. Removing flower stalks before they can set seed and abundant watering over dry periods will prolong bloom. Owing to the shallow, fleshy roots, coralbells is prone to frost heave in winter; during warm spells and in spring the crowns may need to be pushed back into the soil. A loose covering, such as evergreen boughs, helps to alleviate this problem.

Root weevils and mealybugs can be problems, and protection with an insecticide helps. Stem rot can be serious in heavy, wet soils and humid climates.

Coralbells needs rejuvenation by division every fifth or sixth year. When flowering is reduced and clumps have become woody, it is time to divide. Younger plants can be divided for increase, an excellent means of propagation that should be done in spring.

Hibiscus moscheutos

Hosta sieboldiana

Hibiscus moscheutos

(Hy-*bis*-kus)
Rosemallow

Mallow family; native to the marshes of the eastern United States
Height: 5 to 8 feet
Spread: 2 to 2½ feet
Hardy to zone 6

Besides making an effective background of big, bold leaves, the rosemallow produces huge, dramatic flowers. Marginally hardy in northern regions, it is a most useful plant for gardens in the Southwest.

The flowers are red, pink, or white, often with contrasting blotches at the interior of the blossom. The blooms are single, 8 to 12 inches wide, and appear toward the tops of the branched stems. The bloom season is mid-July to frost. Flowering peaks in August, after which the blossoms decrease in size.

The leaves are green on the upper surface, whitish on the lower; oval; and up to 8 inches long. The foliage is dense. The plant is erect to slightly spreading and from 5 to 8 feet high. Despite this height, the leafy stems are

sturdy and rarely require staking. Although they may self-sow in moist soil, rosemallows are generally restrained in growth and not invasive. They are long-lived.

How to start Easy from seed. Soak the seeds in water until they drop to the bottom of the container, then sow outdoors in spring. Germination is very fast, usually within three or four days. The resulting plants usually bloom the next year. Because there is considerable variation from seed, cultivars are best started from divisions in spring. Set the eyes (leaf buds) of the divisions 4 inches below the soil.

Where to plant Rosemallows reach maximum size and lushness in wet, soggy soil high in organic matter, but they also perform well in average, well-drained garden soil. Give them either full sun or partial shade. They are an excellent choice for the southern garden. Space plants 24 to 30 inches apart.

Care Easy. Water abundantly in dry soils. Regular feeding will result in larger, lusher plants. Although

Japanese beetles are attracted to the blossoms, the peak bloom season usually follows the peak beetle season. Leaf spot, canker, rust, blight, aphids, whitefly, and scale can all be problems, although rarely serious. If necessary, protect the plants with a regular insecticide and fungicide program.

Division is never required for rejuvenation but is the best means to increase a favorite cultivar. Divide in either spring or fall.

Hosta sieboldiana

(*Hos*-ta)
Blueleaf plantain lily

Lily family; native to Japan
Height: 2 to 2½ feet
Spread: 2½ to 3½ feet
Hardy to zone 3

Lush, bold foliage is the outstanding feature of this plant. The large, bluish, heart-shaped leaves fan out symmetrically from a central clump. It is an excellent choice for a shady spot.

The flowers are pale lilac to near white. They are like small lilies, 1½ inches long on short, erect stems, and occur

in clusters of 6 to 10 blossoms. Often hidden by the foliage, they bloom in July.

The foliage is bright green when first emerging and assumes a powdery blue cast as the season progresses. The leaves are huge, 10 to 15 inches long and nearly as broad, and somewhat wrinkled on the surface. They grow in a basal rosette and are effective all season long. White- and yellow-variegated cultivars are also available. This long-lived plantain lily freely produces seed, which sometimes germinates, but it could never be called invasive. The variegated cultivars will not breed true from seed.

How to start Set out nursery plants or divisions of young plants in spring. It can be grown successfully from seed, but sizable plants take three years or more to develop and will exhibit considerable variation.

Where to plant Plantain lily tolerates a wide range of soils but is best in well-drained, moist soil high in organic matter. Avoid wet, soggy soils. Either partial or deep

Bed of various types of *Hosta*

Iris 'Dazzling Gold'

shade is satisfactory. Full sun is likely to burn the foliage. Space plants 30 to 36 inches apart.

Care   Easy. The plant needs little attention once established but should be watered deeply and regularly during dry spells. Young plants may profit from a winter mulch, especially if planted in the fall.

Snails and slugs can be quite destructive; use bait for protection. Other chewing insects may also disfigure foliage. Crown rot can be a problem in wet winters if the soil is not well drained.

Plantain lily never requires division and may live 30 years or more in the garden. To propagate, divide only young plants up to three years of age, as older plants develop a tough crown that is hard to separate and even more difficult to establish.

Related species   Many species of *Hosta* abound, ranging in leaf size from a diminutive 2 to 3 inches to the giant just described. Many have showy, sometimes fragrant flowers that add interest to the shady border, and some have variegated cultivars with white or yellow markings.

Hosta decorata (bluntleaf plantain lily) produces 6-inch leaves rimmed with silvery white on compact, 2-foot plants. The flowers are a rich, dark violet, and are showy in August.

H. fortunei (tall-cluster plantain lily) produces many stems bearing showy clusters of small white or pale lavender flowers in August. The oval, light green leaves are 5 to 8 inches long. Several variegated cultivars are available.

H. lancifolia (narrowleaf plantain lily) has slender, 6-inch dark green leaves. It produces great quantities of flower stalks bearing large clusters (up to 30 flowers each) of pale lilac flowers in August.

H. plantaginea (fragrant plantain lily) is a popular old-fashioned favorite with large, 4- to 5-inch fragrant white flowers produced in clusters from mid-August into September. The large, heart-shaped leaves, up to 10 inches long, are light green and form a

mound that can spread to 3 feet.

H. tardiflora (autumn plantain lily) produces large clusters of deep purple flowers just above the leaves. It blooms very late in the season, in October. The plants are small, to 12 inches high and wide, with dainty, dark green, narrow leaves 4 to 6 inches long.

H. undulata (wavyleaf plantain lily) has both fascinating foliage and very showy flowers, with the added advantage of being more tolerant of full sun than any other plantain lily. The leaves have a wavy margin, are striped with white and green, and are relatively small, 6 to 8 inches long. The pale violet flowers are generously produced on stems from 10 to 30 inches tall, and are quite showy in July.

H. ventricosa (blue plantain lily) bears striking blue to deep violet flowers 2 inches long, generously arranged in clusters made up of 10 to 15 flowers. It blooms in July and August. The leaves grow up to 9 inches long and are oval with a delicate twist at the tip.

Iris species
(*Eye*-ris)
Bearded iris

Iris family; most commonly grown varieties are of uncertain hybrid parentage, with parents native around the world, mostly in the northern temperate zones
Height: 4 inches to 4 feet, depending on variety
Spread: 1 to 1½ feet
Hardy to zone 3

Complex hybridization has resulted in a monumental number of iris cultivars to choose from. All have gray-green, swordlike leaves, and their large flowers are available in every color and color combination imaginable. Height ranges from dwarf bearded miniatures 4 to 6 inches tall to the stately, tall plants reaching 4 feet or higher.

The three outer sepals of each flower are called falls; each has a fuzzy central portion called a beard. The three inner petals are called standards and are usually erect and arching. The edges of the falls and petals are often ruffled or laced.

Iris 'Graphic Arts'

Iris 'Broadway'

The vast range of colors and color combinations has resulted in a specialized terminology. Generally, the flowers are divided into five categories.

A *self* is a flower with solid, uniform color.

A *plicata* is generally white or yellow, with contrasting "freckles," or mottling.

A *bicolor* has standards of one color and falls of another, usually darker color. Bicolors have several subclasses, including *amoenas*, which have white standards and colored falls; *reverse amoenas*, with white falls and colored standards; and *variegatas*, which have yellow standards and falls of purple, red, or brown.

Bitones have standards of one color and falls of a different shade of the same color.

Blends are varieties with two or more colors variously intergraded in the same flower parts.

Bearded irises usually bloom for two to three weeks in April, May, or June, depending upon the variety.

The gray-green leaves are held stiffly erect in a fanlike pattern. Tall stalks arise from the foliage, branching at the top to produce blooms on short stems.

The plants spread by rhizomes, producing large, indefinitely expanding clumps that tend to decline and die out in the center unless periodically divided. Each plant rests for a few weeks after blooming, during which time excessive feeding may be detrimental. The leaf tips tend to brown in the summer after blooming, especially in dry years.

How to start Nursery stock or division of rhizomes are the preferred methods. Division should be done after flowering is complete, but not later than mid-August. Separate the rhizomes so that each division has one fan of leaves and several feeder roots. Set the rhizome so that the top is 1 inch below the soil surface, with the newest leaves (and main direction of growth) facing the direction in which you want the plant to grow. Cut the leaves back to 6 inches after planting. Sowing seed is a complex undertaking for those gardeners intrigued by selective breeding.

Where to plant Bearded iris must have well-drained soil, preferably of neutral pH, fertile, and fairly high in organic matter. Give it full sun for the best flowering. Space plants 12 to 15 inches apart.

Care Moderately difficult. Water adequately, but never allow the soil to remain soggy. Tall bearded irises are heavy feeders; feed them once heavily in the early spring and again at about half the strength four or five weeks after blooming has finished. Remove all spent flowers and seed pods regularly.

Iris borer is a serious pest, inflicting severe damage and providing entrance for bacterial soft rot. Begin an insecticide program in spring when leaves are 2 to 3 inches tall, and repeat weekly for the next two to three weeks. Remove and destroy infected rhizomes. Remove old foliage and litter in the fall, as it may harbor borer eggs. Attentive gardeners can note the presence of borers before damage is noticeable. Watch for the trails of slime they leave along the leaf edge before tunneling down through the central portion of a fan into the rhizome.

Divide plants every third or fourth year for rejuvenation. Division is also the best means of increase and is best done just after blooming is complete, when the plant enjoys a brief dormancy. It can also be done in early spring, but this may delay flowering until the following year.

Varieties Several hundred varieties are introduced each year, and available cultivars number in the thousands.

Iris kaempferi

(*Eye*-ris)
Japanese iris

Iris family; native to Japan
Height: 3 to 4 feet
Spread: 1½ to 2 feet
Hardy to zone 4

Massive, stately foliage and huge, flat blossoms distinguish this iris. It is quite finicky about location, but once established in moist, acid soil, it needs little attention for a long, colorful life.

Iris kaempferi

The flowers are white, blue, purple, lavender, and pink. They are often 6 inches or more across. The three overlapping outer falls (see page 84) are large, flat, and held horizontally, and the inner standards are small and spreading. They bloom in late June and July.

The dark green, swordlike leaves often grow 3 to 4 feet tall and remain attractive all season. They are graceful, upright, and slightly arching in clusters topped by tall flowering stems. Flower stems usually grow 3 to 4 feet high, and heights of 6 feet are not uncommon in rich, boggy soil in mild climates.

Japanese iris is restrained in its growth and long-lived. Its rhizomes gradually expand to form a clump.

How to start Nursery stock or division of rhizomes in spring are the accepted methods. Set the divisions 1 inch below the soil level.

Where to plant The soil must be acid, very moist, and well supplied with organic matter. The plant tolerates and even thrives in boggy or frequently flooded areas. Lime and alkaline soil are usually fatal. Give it either full sun or partial shade. Space plants 18 to 24 inches apart.

Care Moderately easy. Water abundantly and maintain acid soil conditions. Feed occasionally with acid plant food. Japanese iris has no serious pests. Division is rarely needed for rejuvenation; most plants can be left undisturbed indefinitely. It is an excellent means of increase, however, and is best done in spring, although it can be done in late summer after flowering.

Related species and varieties Many hybrids are available in white, reddish purple, rose, lavender, blue, violet, purple, and various combinations thereof.

Iris pseudacorus (water flag iris) is another large beardless iris that prefers very moist conditions. The flowers are yellow and appear in great quantities atop 36- to 40-inch stems. This iris will self-sow prolifically in boggy, wet locations and has become naturalized in many such areas in North America.

Iris, **Pacific Coast hybrids**

(*Eye*-ris)
Pacific Coast iris

Iris family; native to coastal western North America
Height: 1 to 1½ feet
Spread: 1 to 1½ feet
Hardy to zone 6, perhaps southern zone 5

The Pacific Coast iris resembles a small Siberian iris, to which it is closely related. The delicate, open blossoms are available in a wide array of colors; the leaves are handsome, grasslike, and evergreen. This iris is most suited to coastal gardens where the summers are mild, especially in the West, where it thrives in the wet winters and dry summers.

The flowers range in color from white to blue, violet, purple, rose, tangerine, orange, yellow, bronze, and brown, usually solid, but sometimes mottled. The falls (see page 84) are frequently wider and more rounded than in the Siberian iris; are held horizontally; and in many varieties are richly veined or blotched with a contrasting color. The standards, rather than being held vertically, open crisply to an angle. The flowers bloom in late March or April in mild climates, in May in more northern areas.

The deep green, linear leaves are arched and rather relaxed in appearance. They are produced singly, rather than in a fan, and form solid, tight, grasslike clumps. They are evergreen and generally handsome all year long, although they may become browned at the tips toward the end of the summer dormancy period.

Pacific Coast iris has many branched flowering stems, which hold the flowers within or slightly above the foliage. Most varieties rarely exceed 12 to 18 inches high.

These irises may occasionally reseed in optimum environments, but they are never invasive. They hybridize freely, and extreme variation will result from plants grown from seed. Pacific Coast iris spreads by surface rhizomes, and its slow growth results in a gradual expansion of the clumps.

Iris, Pacific Coast hybrid 'Amaquita'

How to start   Nursery stock or divisions are preferred. Division is best done in late summer or fall but can be successful in spring just after flowering.

Where to plant   Native to areas of mild, wet winters and temperate, dry summers, they must have perfect drainage and light shade to survive if planted in hot, wet-summer areas. They prefer well-drained soil high in organic matter and of only moderate fertility. In coastal climates, full sun is best. Space plants 10 to 18 inches apart.

Care   These irises require little attention. Fertilize only lightly in early spring. Remove spent flowers and developing seedpods. Do not water during the summer dormancy. The plant has no serious pests. Division is best done in fall (September in the East, October or November in the West), but can also be successful in spring after flowering. It is rarely required for rejuvenation.

Iris sibirica

(*Eye*-ris)
Siberian iris

Iris family; native to central Europe and Russia
Height: 1½ to 3 feet
Spread: 1½ to 2 feet
Hardy to zone 2

Exceptional hardiness, easy culture, long life, and durable, handsome foliage rank the Siberian iris as first-rate for the border or landscape. All have narrow, linear, almost grasslike leaves of various heights that support delicate flowers in June.

Shades of white, blue, and purple are the dominant flower colors. The flowers are smaller and more delicate than those of the bearded iris. The three standards are erect, and the three falls are not bearded (see page 84). The blooms are borne in generous quantities on long stems.

The bright, dark green leaves can be as narrow as ½ inch. They are clean and attractive all season long and appear more relaxed than bearded iris foliage. Erect to arching clumps support many

flower stems, with blossoms visible just above the leaves.

Siberian iris ranges from 18 to 36 inches tall. The small rhizomes and deep, tangled roots expand outward slowly to form dense clumps. The plant seldom needs division, is not invasive, and can be very long-lived.

How to start   Purchase nursery stock or take divisions. Spring is best for division and planting, although it is usually successful throughout the summer.

Where to plant   Siberian iris tolerates a wide range of soils, from extremely moist and rich to very poor and dry. It performs best, however, in moist, fertile soil of slight acidity. Give it full sun to partial shade; it will not flower well in deep shade. Space plants 18 to 24 inches apart.

Care   Easy. Provide abundant moisture and occasional feeding. To improve the plant's appearance, fastidious gardeners often remove spent flowers after blooming is complete. Although the plant is troubled by few pests, the iris borer can be a problem,

contrary to some sources. Dig any infected plants, cut out and destroy the infected portions, and replant the remainder.

Division is rarely necessary for rejuvenation, but occasionally an old clump becomes too crowded and starts dying out in the center. Division can be difficult, as the clumps develop very deep, dense roots. It is an excellent means of increase, however. Division is best done in spring but can be successful up to late summer.

Related species and varieties   Many hybrids of Siberian iris are available, mostly crosses between *Iris sanguinea* and *I. sibirica*. Although too numerous to list here, the numbers are not nearly so overwhelming as are those of bearded iris.

Spuria iris is a class of beardless Eurasian species, some of which grow 4 feet tall. Their rhizomes have a creeping habit and can spread quite wide; they rarely form dense, crowded clumps. *I. orientalis* is the most commonly grown species, with bright yellow, delicate, butterfly blossoms generously produced on 40-

Kniphofia uvaria

Lamiastrum galeobdolon

inch stalks. The leaves are narrow, dark green, and handsome all season, except in hot, dry climates, where they die to the ground in midsummer. Hybrids range in size from 12 inches to 6 feet and display a wide variety of flower colors in white, yellow, blue, violet, and bronze. Spuria irises are generally thought to be more tender than Siberians and may need winter protection north of zone 6.

Kniphofia uvaria
(formerly *Tritoma*)
(Ny-*fo*-fee-a)
Red-hot-poker, torch lily

Lily family; native to southern Africa
Height: 1 to 2½ feet
Spread: 3 to 3½ feet
Hardy to zone 7, some hybrids hardy to zone 5 if mulched in winter

Red-hot-poker produces gracefully arching mounds of grasslike leaves and rigid, erect spikes of brilliant flowers that lend an exotic, almost tropical effect to the garden.

The flowers are flaming red or red-orange, blending into yellow below. The species blooms in August and September, the hybrids in June, July, or August. The hybrids extend and soften the color range from the flaming red and yellow of the species.

The medium- to gray-green foliage forms dense, tufted mounds that either arch gracefully or, in some varieties, are rigid. It is effective all season and is evergreen in mild climates. The mounds are 12 to 30 inches high. From these arise the stiff, vertical "pokers," which can reach from 2 to 4 feet tall.

By producing young offshoots at the outer margins, the clumps expand outward to about 3 to 3½ feet across in four or five years. The plant is long-lived.

How to start   Best purchased as container-grown nursery plants and planted in early spring. Or plant divisions in early spring.

Where to plant   The soil must be well drained; soggy conditions are almost always deadly. Avoid windy spots, as taller spikes may be damaged or broken, and are difficult to stake attractively. Give the plant full sun only. Space plants 18 inches apart.

Care   Easy. Mulch over winter where temperatures drop to 0° F and lower. There are no serious pests. Division may be needed every fourth or fifth year, but most clumps can go indefinitely without disturbance. Divide in early spring for increase.

Varieties   Many varieties are available in white, cream, yellow, gold, pink, coral red, orange, and scarlet. Among the hardiest are 'Earliest of All', coral rose in June; 'Springtime', coral red and white; and 'Summer Sunshine', flame red.

Lamiastrum galeobdolon
(usually listed under its former name *Lamium galeobdolon*)
Yellow-archangel

Mint family; native to Europe
Height: 1 to 2 feet
Spread: 2 feet or more
Hardy to zone 4

Yellow-archangel is a popular creeping ground cover that remains attractive spring through fall, thanks to its silver-mottled, heart-shaped leaves. The hooded flowers are bright yellow and quite showy. It blooms in April.

How to start   Plant divisions or nursery plants in spring.

Where to plant   This extremely tolerant plant grows equally well in sun or shade and in rich or poor soil. It does prefer good drainage. It needs summer watering in hot, dry areas. Space plants 1 to 2 feet apart. It quickly fills in any open spaces.

Care   Very easy. It spreads readily via creeping roots and can be invasive. It is subject to slug damage.

Liatris spicata
(Ly-*ay*-tris)
Blazing-star, gayfeather

Daisy family; native to eastern North America
Height: 2 to 5 feet
Spread: 1 to 1½ feet
Hardy to zone 3

Tall rose, lavender, or purple flower spikes make this plant a useful vertical accent for the

Liatris spicata

Ligularia dentata

garden. Use it either singly in a mixed border or in groups of three or more.

The individual flowers resemble tiny thistle blooms and are packed along the upper 12 to 30 inches of the stems. Blooming in July to September, they open over time from the top of the spike to the bottom.

The dark green, almost grasslike leaves are up to 16 inches long at the base of the plant and become smaller toward the top.

Blazing-star can grow from 2 to 5 feet tall, although 3 feet is most usual in cultivation. Height varies widely depending upon growing conditions and heredity. The plant often self-sows but is seldom invasive. The clumps expand slowly by sending up new stems about the base. It is long-lived.

How to start The easiest method is to sow seeds outdoors in early spring or summer. Seeds must first be prechilled in the refrigerator for several weeks. Germination takes 15 days or more.

Due to variability, named cultivars should be started by divisions made in spring, or from nursery plants.

Where to plant Native to wet meadows and marsh edges in eastern North America, this species responds to moist, well-drained soil high in organic matter and of moderate fertility. In wet locations it may self-sow prolifically. Give it full sun. Space plants 12 to 15 inches apart.

Care Easy. Water abundantly. Removing spent flower spikes may promote a secondary bloom on lateral stems. When cutting a flowering stem, leave two thirds for the plant's food production. This plant has few pests. In areas where the southern root-knot nematode is known to be a problem, don't plant it.

Crowded plants may require division every third or fourth year, but most can go many years without needing rejuvenation. For increase, divide in early spring.

Related species and varieties *Liatris spicata* 'Kobold' is an 18- to 24-inch dwarf with deep purple flowers.

L. scariosa (tall gayfeather) can grow from 18 inches to 5 feet high. 'September Glory', a deep purple in color, and 'White Spires', in white, both have tall flower spikes that open simultaneously instead of gradually from top to bottom. This species is native to sandy prairies and must have very well-drained soil that remains fairly dry over winter.

Ligularia dentata
(Lig-yew-*lay*-ree-a)
Golden groundsel

Daisy family; native to China and Japan
Height: 2 to 4 feet
Spread: 2 to 3 feet
Hardy to zone 4

Large, bold leaves and tall spires of flowers make golden groundsel a useful specimen or border plant. The small flowers are orange-yellow to bright yellow, about 2 inches across, and appear in large quantities held tightly against the tall flower stalks. They bloom in August.

The deep green leaves have a purplish tint. They are broad, rounded, somewhat heart shaped, and grow up to 12 inches across. They are effective all season but may droop and wilt in hot sun or during periods of high heat and humidity.

The plant forms dense basal clumps of leaves up to 18 inches high. From these arise 30- to 40-inch stiffly vertical flower stalks. The plant is fairly restrained in growth and is long-lived.

How to start Divisions or nursery plants in spring are best.

Where to plant Needs moist, rich soil high in organic matter. Dry soils are quickly fatal, but golden groundsel also resents sogginess. Partial shade is best, but the plant takes full sun, especially in cool climates and moist soil. Hot sun causes unsightly drooping of foliage, especially in humid weather. Space plants 24 inches apart.

Care Moderately easy. Water abundantly and feed regularly. Bait for slugs and snails. Division is rarely necessary. It is best done in the spring.

Lobelia cardinalis

Lupinus Russell hybrids

Lobelia cardinalis

(Lo-*bee*-lee-a)
Cardinal flower

Lobelia family; native to
eastern North America
Height: 3 to 4 feet
Spread: 1 to 1½ feet
Hardy to zone 2; does not
perform well in regions with
mild winters

Cardinal flower is a tall,
stately plant with brilliant
scarlet flowers in mid- to late
summer. It is a fine choice for
moist, shady spots, especially
in wild or woodland gardens.

The individual flowers are
small and grow in a spike
along the upper 6 to 8 inches
of the stem. They bloom in
late July to September and attract hummingbirds.

The medium or dark green
leaves are oblong or lance
shaped, growing to 4 inches
long. They are arranged opposite one another or in
whorls along the stalks. The
tall, vertical stems grow 3 to 4
feet high and are topped with
the blazing red flowers.

Unfortunately, the cardinal
flower is short-lived. It self-
sows under optimum con-
ditions, but this is difficult to
rely on. It is seldom, if ever,
invasive.

How to start   It is easiest to
plant nursery stock or sow
seed outdoors in late fall. Or
divide and plant new shoots
that form around the base of
the plant, also in late fall.

Where to plant   Native to
wet soils along streams and in
meadows or to woodland
bottomlands, cardinal flower is
best in well-drained, sandy
loam high in organic matter
and kept evenly moist. Although tolerant of full sun if
kept moist, it does best in
shade or partial shade. Space
plants 12 to 18 inches apart.

Care   Moderately difficult.
Keep the plant well watered.
Remove faded flower stalks.
Mulch in summer to retain
moisture and in winter to protect the crowns. Although several insects and fungal
diseases can attack the plant,
they are seldom serious
enough to warrant protection.
Divide annually to perpetuate
the plant. Lift the clump and
then remove and reset the outside clusters of new basal
growth. This is best done in
early fall.

Lupinus, Russell hybrids

(Loo-*py*-nus)
Russell lupines

Pea family; hybrids of
uncertain parentage
Height: 2 to 4 feet
Spread: 1½ to 2 feet
Hardy to zone 3

These huge, spiky flower
stalks, available in nearly every color and combination of
colors, are unfortunately
adapted only to cool-summer,
humid climates. Where they
can be grown, they are
outstanding either in the
mixed border or massed in
beds all to themselves.

Many types of lupine are
bicolored, and most are available only as mixes. Individually the flowers are pealike
and are arranged in tight
whorls that encircle the stem,
creating clusters that are 1 to
2 feet long. They lend a strong
vertical effect to the garden
when they bloom in June.

The dark green, compound
leaves are from 2 to 6 inches
across and radiate out like the
palm of a hand. Dense with foliage and bushy at the base,
each plant sends up several
flowering spikes.

In favorable climates lu-
pines self-sow profusely, but
the progeny usually revert
back to blue or white colors.
Clumps tend to expand and
crowd, necessitating division,
in those climates where the
plants live long enough.

How to start   Easiest started
from seed, but getting colors
true to type requires hand-
pollinated seed, which can be
expensive. Nick the seed coats
or soak the seeds for 24 hours
prior to sowing. Sow outdoors
in place in spring or late summer, or indoors 8 to 10 weeks
prior to setting out in early
spring. Indoors, they germinate in four to five weeks with
temperatures of 75° F at night
and 80° F during the day.
Move them outside carefully,
as they resent being transplanted. Sowing in peat pots is
the best method. Applying an
inoculant for nitrogen-fixing
bacteria to wetted seeds
reportedly results in more ro-
bust seedlings. The plants also
can be started from nursery
stock or by division.

Where to plant   Best in climates with cool, mild summers
and high humidity. They prefer

Lychnis chalcedonica

Lysimachia clethroides

a neutral, well-drained soil of only moderate fertility. Give them full sun or partial shade. Space plants 18 to 24 inches apart.

Care   Finicky about climate, but otherwise easy. Remove spent flowers before they can set seed. Mulch to retain moisture and keep roots cool. Water over dry periods. A light mulch in areas of harsh winters can be helpful. A regular insecticide and fungicide program will help protect the plant from powdery mildew, rust, aphids, and the fourlined plant bug. Division is rarely necessary, since the plants are short-lived. For increase, divide in early spring.

Lychnis chalcedonica

(*Lik*-nis)
Campion, Maltese-cross

Pink family; native to northern Russia
Height: 2 to 3 feet
Spread: 1 to 1½ feet
Hardy to zone 3

The small flowers of this plant are curiously shaped like a cross. They are brilliant scarlet

and are gathered into dense, rounded clusters atop 2-foot vertical stems. Rose and white cultivars are also available.

The individual flowers are small and five-petaled. They bloom in June and July. Consistent removal of spent flowers will encourage a secondary bloom in August.

The dark green, slightly hairy leaves are held at right angles to the stems. Dense clumps of straight, vertical stems 1 to 2 feet tall support the flower clusters.

Campion reseeds prolifically and can become an invasive nuisance. It is generally short-lived. If it lives long enough, the clump will expand gradually by sending up new shoots around the base. It can become overcrowded and need division.

How to start   Best started from seed sown outdoors in spring, summer, or fall. It will flower the first year if started early indoors, germinating in three to four weeks at a temperature of 70° F. Do not cover the seeds, as they respond to light. Seedlings are difficult to transplant, so start them in peat pots. The plant can also

be started from nursery stock or from divisions made in spring or fall.

Where to plant   The soil must be perfectly drained; wet soil in winter is generally fatal. Give it full sun. Space plants 12 to 15 inches apart.

Care   Moderately difficult. Remove spent flowers to encourage a longer bloom season and a secondary bloom in August. Leaf spot, root rot (particularly in wet winter soil), rust, and smut can all be problems. A regular fungicide program helps. Divide in spring or fall every third or fourth year, as the clumps become overcrowded.

Related species and varieties   *Lychnis coronaria* (rose campion) is a biennial with brilliant magenta flowers produced singly on silvery gray stems and leaves. There is also a white-flowered variety, as well as some that are double-flowered. The plants present an open, stretchy feeling. Although biennial, it self-sows with tremendous vitality. Plant one in your garden and its progeny will be around forever.

L. × *haageana* (Haage campion), despite its hybrid origin, still reproduces well from seed. The flowers are scarlet orange, larger than those of *L. chalcedonica*, and appear singly at the ends of the stems.

Lysimachia clethroides

(Ly-si-*mak*-ee-a)
Gooseneck loosestrife

Primrose family; native to China and Japan
Height: 2 to 3 feet
Spread: 1½ to 2 feet
Hardy to zone 3

Vigorous and easy, this bushy, spreading perennial produces flower spikes shaped like the neck of a goose. The leafy, dense clumps are effective as a low background, and the white flowers are an attractive addition to the late-summer border.

The individual flowers are minute; the spikes are 6 to 8 inches long, and are conical, relaxed, and bent at the ends into a graceful, S-shaped curve. They bloom in July and August.

Lysimachia punctata

Lythrum salicaria

The medium green, slightly hairy leaves are of medium texture and turn an attractive bronze-yellow in the fall. The clumps of erect to slightly spreading stems are bushy and grow to 3 feet high.

The plant spreads rapidly and can become invasive if not divided every year. It is long-lived.

How to start   Easiest started from seed sown in early spring. You can also plant divisions made in spring, or purchase nursery plants.

Where to plant   Best in moist, rich soil high in organic matter. Drier soils are tolerated in partial shade. In moist soils give it full sun or partial shade. Space plants 15 to 24 inches apart.

Care   Easy. Water abundantly. Crown rot and whitefly have been reported as problems. The plant can go for years before needing rejuvenation, but division is usually required every two to four years to restrain the size of the clump. It is best done in the spring.

Related species and varieties   *Lysimachia nummularia* (moneywort) is a low, creeping plant generally reserved as a ground cover. Entirely different in appearance from gooseneck loosestrife, it bears brilliant yellow flowers from June through August. Like its relative, it can be extremely invasive, especially in moist soils and around well-watered lawns. It is very well adapted to wet, boggy conditions and shade.

L. punctata (yellow loosestrife) produces long, 3-foot vertical stems covered with whorls of yellow flowers in June and early July. It can be invasive unless restrained but is a sturdy and reliable plant.

Lythrum salicaria
(*Ly*-thrum)
Purple loosestrife

Loosestrife family; native to Europe
Height: 3 to 5 feet
Spread: 2 feet
Hardy to zone 3

The purple loosestrife is an object lesson in the perils of common names, for it is

unrelated to the previously described plant, gooseneck loosestrife, and also considerably different in appearance and behavior.

Purple loosestrife is a tall, bushy plant that produces erect stems covered with bright flowers nearly all summer. The flowers are pink, magenta, reddish purple, or deep purple. They are produced densely along erect, 12- to 15-inch spikes. They bloom from July to September.

The medium-green leaves are lance shaped and 2 to 4 inches long. They are produced sparsely in whorls along the stems. The stems are strong, almost woody, multi-branched, and erect, growing 3 to 5 feet tall. Flowers appear on the top 8 to 15 inches of the stems. The overall form is a vase shape.

The species reseeds enthusiastically in wet areas. It has naturalized abundantly in the East, frequently choking out large areas of vegetation in swampy areas or around bodies of water. The hybrid cultivars are less rampant, but even the species is usually well behaved in the border.

These plants are long-lived, gradually expanding into large clumps by continually producing basal shoots.

How to start   Easy to start by seed sown in spring or fall. Germination takes about two weeks. The cultivars, which are generally superior, should be started from nursery plants or divisions made in spring. Seed-grown plants will vary considerably.

Where to plant   Although purple loosestrife is best adapted to moist, shady areas, it will perform perfectly well in ordinary garden soil and full sun. Space plants 24 inches apart.

Care   Easy. Water abundantly for the best effect. Removing faded blossoms will improve appearance, possibly extend the flowering season, and prevent self-sowing. The plant has no serious pests. It can go many years before requiring division for rejuvenation. Division is the best means of increase for cultivars. Divide either in spring or fall. Use a sharp knife: The dense, woody roots can be difficult to separate.

Mertensia virginica

Monarda didyma

Mertensia virginica

(Mer-*ten*-sec-a)
Virginia bluebells

Borage family; native to the eastern United States
Height: 1 to 2 feet
Spread: 1 foot
Hardy to zone 3

Virginia bluebells has drooping, bell-shaped flowers that appear in spring. The erect, leafy plants are most attractive in the informal or wild garden.

The outer portion of the petals is sky blue, and the inner part is pinkish or purplish. Each flower is about an inch long, and they are produced in clusters that hang gracefully at the ends of branching stems. They bloom in April and May.

The medium-green leaves are produced both in basal rosettes and alternately along the stems. Leaves are about 8 inches long at the base, becoming smaller as they ascend the stems. All foliage dies back and usually disappears by July.

The stems, which reach 12 to 24 inches high, are gracefully relaxed and curved at the tips. The plant overall is erect and slightly spreading. Long-lasting in suitable locations, Virginia bluebells is restrained in growth and not invasive, but will self-sow here and there.

How to start Easily started from seed sown outside in early spring or fall, from nursery plants, or from the division of dormant roots in early fall. When planting divisions, set the crowns 1 inch below the soil level.

Where to plant Prefers a cool, moist soil high in organic matter and is partial to deep shade. It does best in cool-summer climates of northern latitudes. Space plants 8 to 12 inches apart.

Care Easy in the right location. Keep the soil evenly moist but never soggy. Mulching helps keep soil cool and moist in the summer and also provides a continual supply of decaying organic matter. Do not remove the foliage when it starts to degenerate, but allow it to die down naturally, as you do with bulbs. Some fungal diseases have been reported, but the plant generally is little troubled by disease or pests. Division is seldom required other than for increase. Divide in early fall when roots are dormant.

Monarda didyma

(Mo-*nard*-a)
Beebalm

Mint family; native to the eastern United States
Height: 2 to 3 feet
Spread: 2 feet
Hardy to zone 4

Beebalm's vigorous, bushy clusters of erect stems are topped with fluffy, dense flowers in shades of pink, purple, white, or red. They attract hummingbirds, bees, and butterflies to the garden in profusion. Red-flowered cultivars are especially attractive to hummingbirds. The plant blooms from late June into August.

The dark green, lance-shaped leaves, like other members of the mint family, have a slightly crinkled texture and are aromatic when crushed. They are dense, lush, and remain attractive all season. The dense clumps of erect to slightly spreading stems grow 2 to 3 feet tall.

Beebalm spreads rapidly, sometimes invasively, to form dense mats of fibrous, shallow roots. With age the stems become sparse, lanky, and tall unless regularly divided.

How to start Named varieties are generally superior to the species and are best started from nursery plants or divisions planted in spring. The species is easy to start from seed sown outdoors in spring or fall. Or sow indoors in early spring at 65° F. Germination takes one to two weeks.

Where to plant Best in moist soil high in organic matter and of only average fertility. Give it full sun. In shady locations and rich soil, beebalm can become extremely vigorous and spread rampantly. Space 24 inches apart.

Care Moderately easy. Water abundantly for best appearance, but withhold fertilizer to forestall rapid spreading. Beebalm has few serious pests. In crowded situations with poor air

Oenothera missouriensis

Oenothera berlandieri

circulation, fungus problems, such as powdery mildew and rust, may occur. Although many sources recommend spring division as best, with care beebalm can be moved successfully almost anytime. The clumps will need division every three to four years for containment and rejuvenation. This is also an excellent means of increase.

Varieties 'Cambridge Scarlet' has flaming scarlet flowers and is one of the best and most popular varieties. 'Croftway Pink' has soft, rosy pink flowers that fade to lavender. Other readily available cultivars are 'Snow Queen', with white flowers, and 'Blue Stocking', with light purple flowers.

Oenothera missouriensis
(Ee-no-*thee*-ra)
Ozark sundrops, Missouri primrose

Evening primrose family; native to the central United States
Height: 15 inches
Spread: 2 feet
Hardy in zones 4–9

Ozark sundrops is a popular summer-flowering perennial with stems that first grow upward and then begin to trail. The broad 4- to 5-inch yellow flowers look quite fragile and, indeed, they only last one day, each opening in the evening and closing at the end of the next day. They are, however, borne over a long season, blooming in spring and again in fall.

How to start Best grown from seed sown indoors in spring or outdoors in early summer.

Where to plant This plant is native to dry soils and is subject to rot when conditions are too moist. It does best in sunny, dry sites and tolerates poor soil. It makes a good specimen for low borders. Space plants 2 feet apart.

Care Easy. Spreads moderately when allowed to do so, but without becoming invasive. Self-sown seedlings can be dug out and transplanted elsewhere in the garden.

Related species *Oenothera speciosa* (showy evening primrose), in spite of its common name, is a day-flowering variety. It bears numerous white or pink 2-inch blossoms on upright, 1½-foot stems. It can be quite invasive and is best propagated by division. *O. berlandieri* (Mexican evening primrose) is similar to *O. speciosa*, but with smaller (1½-inch) pink flowers.

Paeonia hybrids
(Pee-*o*-nee-a)
Herbaceous peony

Peony family; the parentage of the many hybrids is uncertain, but most are native to Europe and Asia, a few to North America
Height: 2 to 4 feet
Spread: 3 feet
Hardy to zone 5; does not do well in mild-winter regions

Exceptionally long-lived, with huge, fragrant flowers available in a vast array of colors and forms, as well as glossy foliage that is attractive all season, the peony is considered by many to be indispensable for the border. Its neat, bushy shape and easy culture also make it a valuable addition to the landscape.

Flowers come in shades of pink, white, red, and yellow. They are 3 to 6 inches across, and sit atop long stems. Peonies are superb cut flowers. They bloom in May and June.

Five basic peony flower forms are recognized.

Doubles are fluffy, almost spheroid flowers in which the stamens have developed into fully petallike structures.

Semidoubles are similar, but in these the stamens are not quite so fully developed.

The *Japanese* form is characterized by one or more rows of petals surrounding stamens that carry no pollen and hence are the same color as the petals.

The *anemone* form is similar to the Japanese except that the stamens have been transformed into narrow, petallike parts.

Singles have one or more rows of petals that surround a mass of golden stamens.

The leaves of all peonies are a deep, glossy green, deeply lobed, and medium in texture. The emerging young

Paeonia hybrids

Papaver orientale

shoots are reddish and very attractive in spring; the leaves occasionally develop crimson tints in the fall.

Many leafy shoots appear from a central clump of fleshy roots, creating a bushy, rounded shape that can grow to 3 feet tall. The clumps expand gradually to spread as wide. Peonies are long-lived, orderly, and neat.

How to start   Best from nursery plants or by divisions planted in August or September.

Where to plant   Peonies need a deep, rich, well-drained loam generously amended with organic matter. Full sun is generally best, although light shade is tolerated well. Pastel shades do better in light shade, since the flowers often fade in full sun. Space plants 2 to 3 feet apart when massing, 3 to 4 feet apart as specimens. Peonies apparently require some winter cold and do not do well in mild-winter regions of the Southwest, Southeast, and West Coast.

Care   Usually easy. Water adequately, especially during

dry spells. Feed annually in the spring, but never allow fresh manure or fast-acting nitrogen to directly contact the fleshy roots.

Bait for snails and slugs in the spring, as the emerging shoots are particularly vulnerable. Botrytis and phytophthora blights are the major problems. Practice good garden sanitation by removing and destroying the old foliage in the fall, and prevent water from standing on the foliage in the cool of the evening. Regular applications of a fungicide during bud and bloom may help to prevent botrytis blight.

Division is best accomplished in late August or September. Lift the plants and, with a sharp knife, separate the fleshy roots into segments that each have three to five eyes (the reddish buds visible at the tops of the roots). Plant the sections so that the eyes face up and are exactly 1 inch below the soil surface.

Varieties   Thousands of cultivars are available.

Papaver orientale
(Pap-*ay*-ver)
Oriental poppy

Poppy family; native to Southwest Asia
Height: 2 to 4 feet
Spread: 3 feet
Hardy to zone 2

Oriental poppies produce large, crepe-papery flowers and bold, toothed foliage. They grow best in regions of cool summers and are excellent in conjunction with flowers that bloom later in the summer.

Originally, scarlet-orange was the only color available, but now there is a wide variety of pinks, reds, oranges, and whites. Most varieties have black splotches and black stamens in the center of the blossom. The flowers are from 4 to 10 inches across and have a rumpled texture. They are borne singly on stems 2 to 4 feet tall. They bloom in June.

The light green or grayish leaves are large and hairy. They are dense at the base of the plant, smaller and more scarce higher up. The foliage dies down and disappears in

July and August, but new growth often appears in September and may persist over the winter. The stems have a serpentine, curving quality.

Poppies are fairly long-lived as long as the soil is well drained. The clumps of foliage expand gradually. They should be interplanted with other plants to compensate for the bare spots left by the dying foliage.

How to start   Best from nursery plants or divisions. Plant divisions from August to early September. Set the root crowns 3 inches below the soil level. Mulch lightly over the first winter, but avoid suffocating the young crowns.

Where to plant   The plant must have well-drained soil; wet crowns, particularly in winter, are usually fatal. Adding organic matter can be beneficial, but the soil should be of only average fertility. It performs best in regions of cool summers and is short-lived in warm-winter climates. Give it full sun or partial shade. Space plants 15 to 20 inches apart.

Penstemon hartwegii

Phlox paniculata

Care   Moderately easy, given excellent drainage. A summer mulch will help keep the soil cool and the roots moist. Take care not to damage roots with cultivation in late summer after the foliage has died down. Plants with tall stems probably will require staking.

Avoid letting water stand on leaves and crowns on cool days or overnight, as this invites bacterial blight and downy mildew. Aphids may present a problem, as may the northern root-knot nematode.

Oriental poppies will require division every four or five years for rejuvenation. This is best done in August or early September.

Varieties   More than sixty cultivars are available.

Penstemon hartwegii

(Pen-*stee*-mon)
Beardtongue

Snapdragon family; native to Mexico
Height: 1 to 3 feet
Spread: 1 to 1½ feet
Hardy to zone 7

Beardtongue produces colorful, trumpetlike blossoms of rose, pink, lavender, or white that

are vaguely reminiscent of snapdragon or foxglove. Members of the *Penstemon* genus grow naturally from Oregon to Chile.

The flowers are tubular and nod on slender stalks. They bloom in June and July.

The medium-green, lance-shaped leaves are 2 to 4 inches long. The stems are vertical, branching at the base.

Somewhat delicate in nature, beardtongue generally is not long-lived. It self-sows in a favorable climate, but the seedlings are extremely variable.

How to start   Purchase nursery plants or sow hand-pollinated seeds outdoors in late summer. Seeds can be sown indoors in early spring at 65° F. Germination usually takes less than a week. Division in spring is possible but difficult.

Where to plant   The soil must be well drained and gritty, and preferably on the acid side (pH 5.5 to 6.5). Full sun is best, but it tolerates light shade. Space plants 12 to 18 inches apart. Beardtongue should be considered only for mild, coastal climates.

Care   Moderately difficult; beardtongue is very picky about location. Do not overwater, but be sure to water during droughts. Most members of the genus are native to mild-winter, dry-summer climates of the Mediterranean and the western Americas. To prevent seed formation, cut the stems after flowering. Do not overfertilize. Mulch over winter to protect from cold. Beardtongue has no serious pests, although leaf spot and rust have been reported. A fungicide is an effective protection. Though difficult to transplant, many cultivars require division every other year to look their best. This is best done in early spring.

Phlox paniculata

(Flox)
Summer phlox, garden phlox

Phlox family; native to the eastern United States
Height: 2 to 4 feet
Spread: 2 feet
Hardy to zone 3

Masses of color and a stately presence are the hallmarks of this perennial phlox. Equally characteristic is the need for

spraying, staking, frequent watering and dividing, and weeding out self-sown seedlings. Despite the work in raising phlox well, many gardeners consider it indispensable for the border.

Flowers come in red, pink, salmon, magenta, purple, lavender, and white. Individually they are like discs about 1 inch across and are gathered into massive conical or hemispherical flower heads 10 to 14 inches across. They usually bloom from July to early September, but this varies according to cultivar.

The dark green leaves are lance shaped and about 3 to 5 inches long. The 2- to 4-foot-high stems are dense with foliage, each topped with a large flower head.

Phlox self-sows prolifically, but the seedlings of cultivars are not true to type; many revert back to their original magenta. This is a relatively short-lived plant. It requires thinning out of old growth annually and division every third year.

How to start   Best results are obtained from nursery plants or divisions made in

Phlox subulata

Platycodon grandiflorus

either spring or fall. Most cultivars purchased at nurseries are root cuttings. Sow seed in the fall.

Where to plant The soil should be deep, moist, well drained, high in organic matter, and very fertile. It is best to add superphosphate generously to the soil when planting. Full sun is best, although phlox tolerates partial shade. Provide a location with good air circulation, but avoid windy spots. Space plants 24 inches apart.

Care Difficult for a presentable appearance. Water abundantly, especially during drought, but do so early in the day and preferably from below to avoid getting water on the foliage. Fertilize regularly. Remove the flower heads by snapping them off just below the last flower to encourage the formation of lateral buds and more flowers. It also discourages reseeding. Phlox requires staking.

Powdery mildew and rust, as well as red spider mites in hot, dry weather, are the worst problems. Spray with an insecticide and a fungicide

every 10 to 14 days throughout the season.

Divide every third year to rejuvenate, replanting only the healthiest outer shoots of the clump. This should be done in either spring or fall.

Related species *Phlox subulata* (moss pink) is an entirely different plant in appearance and care. It is low and mat forming with bright green, dense, needlelike, evergreen leaves. It makes an excellent ground cover or bed in full sun and light, sandy soil. In April it is covered with flowers in shades of pink, white, red, or lavender. The hues are usually of electric intensity. Moss pink is hardy to zone 3.

Platycodon grandiflorus
(Plat-i-*ko*-don)
Balloon-flower

Harebell family; native to eastern Asia
Height: 2 to 3 feet
Spread: 1½ feet
Hardy to zone 3

The balloon-flower is a long-lived and easy perennial

whose bell-shaped blossoms resemble small inflated balloons when in bud.

Its flowers come in shades of blue (the usual color), white, and pink. They are 2 to 3 inches across and appear at the ends of long stems on the upper part of the plant. They bloom in July and August, and often into early September.

The leaves are medium green with a bluish cast to the underside. They are oval to lance shaped, 1 to 3 inches long, and grow densely against the stems. The bushy clusters of erect stems are 2 to 3 feet tall. The flowers appear above and within the foliage.

Balloon-flower is restrained in growth and long-lived. It is slow to appear in the spring, so be careful with early cultivation. It's wise to put in a plant marker to mark its place before it disappears for the winter. It is also slow to reach maturity; the full effect is seldom achieved before three years.

How to start The plant can be started from seed, but flowers will not appear for two to

three years. Sow seeds in spring or late summer, and do not cover them with soil. Divisions give faster results, but transplanting can be difficult. Cut off the outer sections of the thick crown, retaining as many buds and roots as possible, and plant these divisions thickly to safeguard against some failures. Set the crowns so that they are barely covered with soil.

Where to plant Light, fluffy, sandy, well-drained soil is best. The plant tolerates many soils but will not take wet soil in winter. Give it either full sun or partial shade. Space plants 12 to 18 inches apart.

Care Easy. The plant responds to adequate watering, but does flower well in hot, dry locations. Removing faded flowers extends the bloom season. Tall plants may require staking. Balloon-flower has no serious pests. Fortunately, the plants are long-lived and never require division for rejuvenation. Division is often difficult and usually gives erratic results. Dividing is best done in spring.

Polygonatum commutatum

Primula cockburniana

Polygonatum commutatum

(Po-lig-o-*nay*-tum)
Great Solomon's-seal

Lily family; native to eastern
North America
Height: 3 to 4 feet
Spread: 1½ to 3 feet
Hardy to zone 4

This woodland native has long,
attractive, arching stems and
hanging clusters of tiny flowers. It is one of those rare
plants that likes dry shade.

The flowers are yellowish
green to greenish white, about
½ inch long, bell shaped, and
droop in small clusters all
along the undersides of the
stems. They bloom in May and
early June.

Foliage is the chief attrac-
tion of this plant. The deep,
rich green to bluish green
leaves grow up to 7 inches
long. They are held perpendicular to the stem and alternate
along its length.

The stems often reach 3 to
4 feet in length. The plant
spreads slowly by rhizomes
and can form broad patches in
time. It is long-lived and not
invasive.

How to start   Purchase
nursery plants or take divisions. Plant divisions in
early spring or after flowering
is complete.

Where to plant   Great
Solomon's-seal is best grown in
cool, moist soil well amended
with organic matter. However,
it tolerates dry soil and inten-
sive root competition well.
Give it deep to partial shade.
Space 18 to 36 inches apart.

Care   Easy to moderately
easy. Water adequately and
mulch over summer. It has no
serious pests. Although never
required for rejuvenation, division for increase is easy
when done in early spring.

Primula vulgaris

(*Prim*-yew-la)
English primrose

Primrose family; native
to Europe
Height: 3 inches to 3 feet
Spread: 6 to 15 inches
Hardy to zone 5

Primula is a complex and var-
ied genus of several hundred
species, varying in height from
a few inches to as tall as 3

feet. Most bloom in April or
May in northern climates and
as early as February in mild
climates.

In general, primroses form
basal rosettes of attractive,
often crinkly, and sometimes
evergreen leaves. From the foliage arise vertical flower
stalks bearing single flowers,
heads, or clusters of flowers
sometimes arranged in tiers.
The flowers in the genus occur
in all colors. *Primula vulgaris* and its hybrids are
among the easiest to grow.

The flowers of English
primrose are pale yellow. Hybrids are available in a wide
range of nearly every color except pure red and pure blue.
The flowers are about 1 inch
across and are held one to a
stalk just above the leaves.
Prolific in bloom, a mature
clump may produce more than
a hundred flowers over a two-
month period.

The bright green leaves are
tonguelike and produced in
low basal rosettes, usually flat
against the ground. They are
evergreen where temperatures
do not drop below 15° F. Short
flowering stalks grow from the
center of the rosette.

Plants may go dormant in
summer drought and reemerge
in autumn. They self-sow in
favorable environments but
are never invasive. Like most
other primroses, this one
spreads vegetatively, sending
up new plantlets by way of
surface roots near the crown.
English primrose is fairly long-
lived. Divide frequently to
maintain vigor.

How to start   Easily grown
from nursery bedding plants
or from seed sown in late winter or early spring on the surface of a moist, peaty soil mix.
The seeds require light to
germinate and need humidity,
so cover the flat with clear
plastic. The plant is also easy
to start from divisions made in
spring after flowering is over,
or in autumn.

Where to plant   Although
many species are quite hardy,
primroses grow best in mild,
humid climates that do not
have extreme summer or winter temperatures. Most primroses, including this species,

Primula vulgaris

Pulmonaria saccharata

should have rich, deep, moist, well-drained soil high in organic matter. Partial shade, preferably the shade of high tree branches, is best. Protection from hot afternoon sun is essential. Space plants 6 to 15 inches apart.

Care Moderately easy. Although particular about location, this is one of the easiest primroses to grow. Water abundantly, especially during dry spells. Adding organic matter yearly by mulching over winter should provide all the nutrition it needs. Slugs and snails can be a problem. Divide clumps every third year, after flowering in the spring or in the fall. Division is easy, and the plant quickly reestablishes itself.

Related species *Primula × polyantha* (polyanthus primrose) is the result of crosses made between *P. vulgaris* and several other species. This group is characterized by large, bold blooms, several to a stem, in a huge array of bright colors. Not as long-lived as *P. vulgaris*, they require essentially the same care. Division may be needed

every other year, and occasional fertilizing is beneficial. In hot, dry weather, red spider mites can be a serious problem. Hardy to zone 5.

P. japonica (Japanese primrose) is quite different in appearance, producing several tiers, or whorls, of magenta, pink, or white flowers along 2-foot stems. Like most of the candelabra types, it requires a very moist or boggy soil and can be difficult to grow if conditions are not exactly right. The blossoms begin to appear in May and often last through June. Other candelabra primroses are *P. burmanica* and *P. beesiana,* both having purple flowers; *P. bulleyana* and *P. helodoxa,* yellow flowers; and *P. cockburniana* and *P.* 'Pagoda' hybrids, orange flowers. All require similar culture.

P. sieboldii has bright green, wrinkled leaves with scalloped edges and clusters of lilac-pink flowers on 6- to 9-inch stems in late spring. Hybrids are available in many shades of white, pink, and purple, including bicolors.

Pulmonaria saccharata

(Pul-mo-*nay*-ree-a)
Lungwort; Bethlehem sage

Borage family; native
to Europe
Height: 6 to 8 inches
Spread: 10 inches
Hardy to zone 4

Lungwort's deep green leaves speckled with white make an attractive ground cover in the shade. Small flowers in early spring are an extra advantage, and it is easy to grow.

Flowers come in blue, reddish violet, or white. Individually they are trumpetlike and about ½ inch long. They appear in clusters on stalks 10 to 12 inches tall. The flowers are often pink in bud, changing to blue as they open. They bloom in early April and May.

The exceedingly attractive, glossy leaves are oval to heart shaped and grow to about 6 inches long. The basal rosettes of leaves reach 6 to 8 inches in height. From the crown arise several flowering stalks. The foliage remains attractive all season long.

The plant is long-lived, slow growing, and not invasive.

How to start Purchase nursery plants or make divisions in fall or very early spring. Until the ground freezes, keep fall-planted divisions heavily watered.

Where to plant Moist soil high in organic matter is best, although it need not be fertile. Give these plants partial to deep shade. Space them 10 inches apart.

Care Easy. The plant requires little attention. Watering over dry spells is beneficial. It has no serious pests. Although seldom required, division is an excellent means of increase. It is best done in late summer or very early spring, although success is common even during full bloom. Water heavily after transplanting.

Related species and varieties *Pulmonaria saccharata* 'Mrs. Moon' is a form with larger flowers that are pink in bud and bright blue when open.

P. angustifolia (blue lungwort) has plain, dark green leaves that are quite hairy,

Rudbeckia fulgida

Salvia × *superba*

almost bristly. The flowers are showy, pink in bud, opening to blue, and appear in April and May. Several varieties are available, including pink, salmon, white, and red ones. Some sources list these under *P. saccharata*.

Rudbeckia fulgida var. *sullivantii* 'Goldsturm'

(Rood-*bek*-ee-a)
Goldsturm black-eyed-susan

Daisy family; native to eastern North America
Height: 2½ feet
Spread: 1 to 2 feet
Hardy to zone 4

Unlike many other members of this genus, this is a true, long-lived perennial. The deep yellow daisies of this plant are produced in great quantities over a long season in late summer. This cultivar is probably the best for its profuse bloom and its even, 2½-foot growth.

The flowers are deep yellow with a black central "cone." They are 3 to 4 inches across and nearly cover the plant over a long season, blooming from mid-July to mid-September. The cones persist and are attractive well into winter.

The dark green leaves are lush and dense. The multi-branched stems are erect and spreading. The overall form is a vase shape. The flowers are produced at the ends of the branches, often covering the foliage. Unlike most other *Rudbeckia* species, the foliage of this one remains clean and attractive all season.

Most black-eyed-susans are weedy self-sowers and short-lived to boot. This one is neither. 'Goldsturm' has a restrained growth that lasts for years in the garden. The clumps expand gradually, sending up new shoots at the outer edges.

How to start   Nursery plants or division in spring are best. Fall planting, too, is generally successful.

Where to plant   Prefers well-drained, moist soil of average fertility. Black-eyed-susan likes full sun; in shade it has a more open habit and produces fewer flowers. Space 12 to 24 inches apart.

Care   Easy. The plant requires little attention and never needs staking. Water over dry periods. Aphids may be a problem but are easily controlled with an insecticide. Downy mildew, rust, and powdery mildew can be controlled with a fungicide. Division is best performed in spring but is usually successful in fall as well. Most clumps need dividing every fourth or fifth year to maintain their vigor.

Related species and varieties   *Rudbeckia hirta* var. *pulcherrima* 'Gloriosa Daisy' is often sold as a perennial, although in nearly all cases it behaves as a self-sowing annual.

R. laciniata 'Goldquelle' is like *R. fulgida* 'Goldsturm', except slower growing and with double flowers.

R. nitida 'Herbstonne' (often listed as *R. nitida* 'Autumn Sun') grows 4 to 5 feet tall on strong stems that do not require staking. The flowers are deep yellow with brown centers, about 3 or 4 inches across, and are produced in generous quantities in late summer.

Salvia × *superba*

(formerly *S. nemorosa*)
(*Sal*-vee-a)
Perennial salvia

Mint family; parents native to the Mediterranean region
Height: 2 to 3 feet
Spread: 1 to 2 feet
Hardy to zone 5 and farther north when mulched in winter

Spikes of violet-purple flowers and gray-green foliage that last throughout the season make this plant a welcome addition to the mixed border or individual beds.

The individual flowers are tiny and densely whorled around the spikes, which are 4 to 8 inches long. They bloom in June or August and are surrounded by red-violet bracts that persist after the flowers are finished, providing a long, colorful season. The blooms are good for cut flowers and for drying for winter arrangements.

The leaves are of medium texture and effective all season long. They are aromatic when crushed. The multi-branched stems are densely clothed in leaves, and the plant grows 2 to 3 feet tall.

Scabiosa caucasica

Scabiosa caucasica 'David Wilkie'

Perennial salvia can be long-lived if conditions are favorable, especially if the soil is well drained. It stays in place and, since it is sterile, never self-sows.

How to start Purchase nursery plants or plant stem cuttings or divisions in spring.

Where to plant The soil must be well drained. Give it full sun. It will withstand heat, drought, and poor soil well. Wet soil in winter is usually fatal. Space plants 1 to 2 feet apart. An excellent choice for the southern states.

Care Easy in the right location. Remove spent flowers to prolong the bloom period. Leaf spot, rust, scale, and whitefly can be minor problems. Division is best done in spring. The root system is long and stringy, and reestablishment is usually slow. Fortunately, division is rarely required for rejuvenation. In northern zones apply a protective mulch after the soil freezes.

Related species and varieties *Salvia azurea* (azure sage) is a large, 4- to 5-foot plant with intense gentian blue flowers in late summer

and early fall. It needs staking and is hardy only to zone 6. The variety *grandiflora*, often listed in catalogs as *S. pitcheri*, has deeper, more brilliant blue flowers.

S. pratensis (meadow clary), formerly *S. haematodes*, has lavender-blue flowers arising above a basal clump of foliage. It blooms in June. Because it has a tendency to behave like a biennial, it is wise to set out new plants yearly to perpetuate it in the garden.

Scabiosa caucasica

(Skab-i-*o*-sa)
Pincushion-flower

Teasel family; native to the Caucasus
Height: 2 to 2½ feet
Spread: 1 to 1½ feet
Hardy to zone 2

The pincushion-flower's pastel blue, sometimes white, flowers on open, branching stems bloom nearly all summer long. Seldom planted as a focal specimen on its own, it is an asset to the mixed, informal border.

The pale blue petals surround protruding gray stamens

that resemble pins in a pincushion. Growing to 3 inches across and appearing at the ends of the stems, they bloom from June to September.

The medium-green basal leaves are oblong to lance shaped and measure up to 5 inches. The stem leaves are toothed and smaller. The foliage is large and dense at the base of the plant, becoming smaller and more sparse on the stems. The stems are upright and arching, and grow in clusters, giving it an open, loose appearance.

With periodic division, this is a relatively long-lived plant. It is restrained in habit. Clumps expand gradually by sending up shoots at the outer perimeter.

How to start Sow purchased seed in early spring or sow indoors at 65° F. Germination takes one to two weeks. It may bloom some by the end of the first season. Or sow freshly collected, ripe seed outdoors in early fall. You can also purchase nursery stock or plant divisions in spring.

Where to plant Because summer drought and winter

sogginess are both fatal, the plant requires the hard-to-achieve combination of perfect drainage and moist soil. Sandy loam generously amended with organic matter is best. Give it full sun. Space plants 10 to 15 inches apart.

Care Moderately easy. Mulch in summer and water over dry periods. Deadhead to prolong blooming. Mulching over winter is recommended in harsh climates. There are few serious pests, but mildew and root rot have been reported. The clumps may start to degenerate in the third or fourth year, requiring division to restore vigor. This is also an excellent means of increase and should be done in the spring.

Sedum spectabile

(*See*-dum)
Showy stonecrop,
showy sedum

Stonecrop family; native to China and Japan
Height: 2 feet
Spread: 1 foot
Hardy to zone 3

These mounded, 2-foot plants have fleshy, light green leaves

Sedum spectabile 'Autumn Joy'

Solidago 'Gold Schleier'

topped with many flat clusters of flowers from August to frost. They are especially effective massed in the border or in beds by themselves.

The flowers are various shades of pink, rose, and white, turning to bronze as they mature and developing fruit in the fall. Individually they are tiny and produced in dense, flat-topped or hemispherical clusters 3 to 4 inches across, often covering the top of the plant. Most *Sedum* species attract butterflies. They bloom from early August to the middle of September. The bronze fruit is attractive well after frost.

The light green leaves often appear dusted with white and are thick, fleshy, and rounded. Growing to about 3 inches across, they are arranged either opposite one another or whorled against the succulent stems.

Clusters of many upright to spreading stems are densely clothed with leaves, each stem ending in a flat flower cluster. Neat and tidy, the overall form is mounded, growing 18 to 24 inches high. The foliage is attractive all season.

The clumps expand by producing new shoots. In very rich soils they have a tendency to spread apart, revealing an open center. The showy stonecrop is a long-lived plant and is never invasive.

How to start   Nursery plants and divisions are best planted in spring. Stem cuttings root easily and should be made in summer. Seeds can be sown in late summer or mid-spring at 65° F. Hybrids do not breed true from seed.

Where to plant   Members of the *Sedum* genus are not fussy about soil as long as it is well drained. This group needs moist soil, richer than that required by other *Sedum* species, and will grow in quite wet soil. Give the plants full sun; partial shade is best in hot climates. Space plants 12 to 18 inches apart.

Care   Easy. Showy stonecrop responds to adequate water. It has no serious pests. Although the plant can go many years without requiring division for rejuvenation, division is an excellent means of increase and is best done in spring.

Solidago hybrids

(Sol-i-*day*-go)
Goldenrod

Daisy family; although the parentage is uncertain, most are probably from Europe and the eastern United States
Height: 1½ to 3½ feet
Spread: 1 to 1½ feet
Hardy to zone 3

Much successful hybridizing has resulted in outstanding golden yellow color on sturdy, easily grown plants. Contrary to popular belief, goldenrod does not cause hay fever. Its heavy, waxy pollen is insect borne and never travels on the wind. The insidious hay fever-causing ragweeds (*Ambrosia* species) bloom at approximately the same time. This has led to the blame falling to the lot of the more conspicuous, but innocent, goldenrod.

Goldenrod flowers appear in various shades of yellow, from primrose and canary to dark gold. Individually they are tiny, but they are produced in great quantities in flat-topped clusters, or along flower stalks held perpendicular to the stem. They bloom in August and September.

The medium-green, lance-shaped leaves are held tightly against the upright stems. The branching, upright or slightly spreading stems grow in clusters, 18 to 40 inches tall and generally in a vase shape.

Goldenrod is long-lived, restrained in growth, and never invasive. It slowly increases by sending up shoots along the outside perimeter of the clump.

How to start   Plant nursery plants or divisions either in spring or fall.

Where to plant   Goldenrod is quite adaptable to most any soil, although very wet or very dry ones should be avoided. Give it full sun. Space plants 12 to 15 inches apart.

Care   Easy. The tallest varieties may require staking if grown in rich soils. The plant has no serious pests. It can go for years without needing division for rejuvenation. To increase, divide in spring or late fall.

Stachys officinalis

Stokesia laevis

Stachys byzantina
(*Stay*-kis)
Lamb's-ears, woolly betony

Mint family; native to Turkey
and southwestern Asia
Height: 6 to 12 inches
Spread: 24 inches
Hardy to zone 4

Lamb's-ears is a low, tufted
plant grown for its outstanding foliage. The leaves are
densely woolly and an intense
silvery white. In the front of
the border it makes an eye-
catching accent, particularly
on moonlit nights. It is especially attractive combined
with pastel shades of blue and
pink flowers.

The flowers of lamb's-ears
are purplish white. They
bloom from July through
September and are pleasant
but not particularly showy.
The plant is grown primarily
for its foliage. ('Silver Carpet'
is a nonflowering form.)

The leaves grow to an
oblong or tonguelike shape 4 to
6 inches long. They are arranged in low radial clumps 6
to 12 inches high and often
spread 24 inches wide. Lamb's-
ears can be quite long-lived
but is usually neat and

restrained in its growth. The
clumps expand slowly, but after several years they begin to
die out in the center, necessitating division.

How to start Nursery plants
or division in spring are the
usual methods, but this plant
is easy to start from seed sown
outdoors in mid-spring or indoors in early spring at 65° F.
Germination usually takes less
than a week.

Where to plant The soil
must have perfect drainage
and should be of only moderate fertility. Lamb's-ears
tends to rot in damp, humid
climates. Give it full sun.
Plant 10 to 15 inches apart.

Care Moderately easy. Avoid
overwatering. There are no
serious pests. Divide after the
fourth year to rejuvenate. Division is also an excellent
means of increase.

Related species *Stachys
grandiflora* (big betony) is a
taller, bushy plant with grayish green leaves. It produces
great quantities of bright
purple flowers that are 1 inch
long and gathered in whorls
around tall spikes. They bloom
in May and June. The flowers

are beloved by bees. The plant
grows best in partial shade.

S. officinalis is similar to
big betony but with smaller,
less impressive flowers. It produces tall, whorled flower
spikes of rosy purple in July
and August. It is best in full
sun and a dry soil.

Stokesia laevis
(*Stokes*-ee-a)
Stokes' aster

Daisy family; native to South
Carolina south to Louisiana
and Florida
Height: 1 to 1½ feet
Spread: 1 to 1½ feet
Hardy to zone 6

The flowers of this perennial
resemble a cross between an
aster and a pincushion-flower.
They are most effective when
grown in small groups in the
mixed border.

The flowers are lavender
to silvery or dark blue, and
sometimes pure white. Like a
daisy, they have an outer single or double row of "petals"
or, more accurately, ray florets, and a center of fuzzy-
looking disc florets in the

same color. They are produced
singly blooming in July and
August.

The narrow, dark green,
lance-shaped leaves can grow
to 8 inches long. Large basal
clumps of leaves support many
flower stalks. Stokes' aster can
be long-lived if the soil is perfectly drained in winter. The
clumps often get crowded by
the fourth year, requiring
division.

How to start The plant is
easy to start from seed sown
outdoors in April. Nursery
plants or clump divisions can
also be planted in the spring.

Where to plant Stokes' aster is absolutely intolerant of
wet soil in winter, so fast
drainage is essential. Otherwise, it is not too fussy about
soil. Give it full sun. Space
plants 12 to 15 inches apart.

Care Moderately difficult,
being very touchy about soggy
soil in winter. Otherwise, it requires little special attention.
There are no serious pests. Division is required about every
four years to reduce crowding.
Division is also a good means
of increase and is best done in
the spring.

Thalictrum aquilegifolium

Thermopsis caroliniana

Thalictrum rochebrunianum

(Thal-*ik*-trum)
Lavender-mist meadowrue

Buttercup family; native
to Japan
Height: 3 to 6 feet
Spread: 2 feet
Hardy to zone 5

These tall, airy plants have
finely textured foliage topped
with delicate sprays of lavender flowers. Growing 3 to 6
feet high or more, this
meadowrue makes a splendid
background plant.

The flowers are lavender-
violet with bright yellow stamens. Individually they are
minute and have no petals; the
showy parts are the purplish
sepals and yellow stamens.
They appear in great quantities in July and August.

The very delicate, medium-
green leaves often have a bluish cast. They are compound,
with many small three-leaf
leaflets. An open, lacy appearance belies strong stems that
never require staking. The foliage effect is similar to that
of maidenhair fern, with
which the plant is often
compared.

Meadowrue grows slowly
and is long-lived. New divisions may take two or three
seasons to fill out.

How to start   Sow seeds outdoors in the fall. Fresh seed
will germinate best. Seed can
be sown in spring if given a
three- to five-week period of
prechilling in the refrigerator,
but germination is often erratic. Nursery plants or divisions planted in spring are
preferable, although fall plantings are usually successful
with winter protection.

Where to plant   The plant
prefers deep, rich, moist soil
high in organic matter. Partial
shade is best, but it will tolerate full sun if the soil is kept
moist. Space 24 inches apart.

Care   Moderately easy.
Meadowrue appreciates abundant water. It has few serious
pests, but powdery mildew and
rust are occasionally reported.
It is best to divide the plant
about every fifth year to relieve crowding. An excellent
means of increase, this can be
done either in spring or fall.

Divisions planted in fall
should be mulched to protect
them over winter.

Related species   *Thalictrum aquilegifolium* (columbine meadowrue) has
fluffy, pinkish purple flowers
that are effective from late
May to early June on 3-foot
stems. Rose and white varieties are also available. The
grayish green foliage resembles columbine in both texture
and color. More widely grown
than *T. rochebrunianum*, it
is smaller and less refined.

Thermopsis caroliniana

(Ther-*mop*-sis)
False-lupine

Pea family, native from North
Carolina to Georgia
Height: 3 to 4 feet
Spread: 2 to 3½ feet
Hardy to zone 3

Resembling a tall, slender, yellow lupine, with its spikes of
pealike flowers, false-lupine
will withstand the hot, muggy
summers of the Southeast. It is
also easy and completely
hardy elsewhere in the United
States. Relatively unknown,

it may be difficult to locate
commercially.

The individual flowers are
small and are gathered into
10- to 12-inch spikes atop erect
stems. They bloom in June and
early July.

The dark green leaves are
divided into three leaflets. The
plant forms clusters of rigidly
upright stems clothed in leaves
and tipped with flower spikes.

False-lupine is long-lived
and restrained in growth. It
seldom needs division. Early to
appear and fast-growing in the
spring, the foliage remains
lush and dense all season long.

How to start   Easy to start
from seed sown in late summer. Before sowing, soak the
seeds in warm water or file
the seed coats. The plant can
also be started from nursery
plants or clump divisions
planted in late summer.

Where to plant   Prefers
well-drained soil of poor to
average fertility. Like most
members of the pea family, its
root nodules fix nitrogen from
the atmosphere. As a result,
false-lupine almost never
needs fertilizing, and soil that
is excessively rich in nitrogen

Tradescantia viginiana

Trillium erectum

makes the leaves turn yellow. Full sun is best, although it tolerates partial shade well. Space plants 24 to 40 inches apart.

Care Easy. Some staking is probably necessary in windy areas. It has no serious pests. Division is rarely required for rejuvenation, which is fortunate, since old clumps are difficult to divide because of the dense, deep roots. Division is frequently unsuccessful; if you attempt it, do so in late summer.

Tradescantia virginiana

(Trad-es-*kant*-ee-a)
Spiderwort

Spiderwort family; native to the eastern United States
Height: 1½ to 3 feet
Spread: 1½ to 2½ feet and beyond
Hardy to zone 4

Adaptable to many difficult situations, including infertile soil, deep shade, and boggy conditions, the spiderwort provides small, colorful flowers over a long season. It has, however, a tendency to sprawl and ramble through the garden unless restrained. Named cultivars are usually superior to the native species.

The flowers are usually bright purple, although many varieties have been selected that are white, blue, purple, pink, or red. The blossoms are composed of three petals, are about 1 inch wide, and each lasts only a day; they are produced in clusters at the ends of the stems and bloom from June to September.

The deep green leaves are almost straplike, growing to 1 inch wide and as long as 15 inches. The lower portion of the leaf is wrapped around the stem, giving the plant the appearance of a coarse grass. The form is variable but mostly upright, and the plant is from 18 to 36 inches high. The stems are angled at the joints. From midseason on, the plant tends to sprawl.

Spiderwort spreads enthusiastically by underground stems as well as by aboveground stems that root where their joints contact the soil. It is long lived but requires frequent division to restrain rampant growth.

How to start The species is easy to start by seed sown in the spring, but best results will occur from fresh seed collected and sown in late summer. Germination takes about two weeks. Nursery plants or divisions of named cultivars should be planted in spring.

Where to plant Spiderwort tolerates nearly any soil but grows most vigorously in moist, rich ones. Gardeners desiring to restrain the plant's growth should avoid planting it in rich, moist soils. It takes full sun to deep shade. Space plants 15 to 30 inches apart.

Care Easy. Spiderwort looks best with adequate water. If the stems flop badly in midsummer, cut them to the ground; the plant will flower again in the fall.

The plant has few serious pests, although several caterpillars have been reported. Botrytis blight may attack the blossoms.

Division is best performed every other year. It is an excellent means of increase and should be done in spring.

Trillium grandiflorum

(*Trill*-ee-um)
Wakerobin, snow trillium

Lily family; native to northeastern North America
Height: 12 to 18 inches
Spread: 12 inches
Hardy to zone 5

Wakerobin is a striking woodland plant with pure white flowers fading to pink. The blooms are composed of three broad petals and measure 3 to 6 inches across. Each sturdy, upright stem bears a single set of leaves, likewise borne in threes. They are broad and wavy with conspicuous veins. Wakerobin blooms in late March and April. All aboveground parts of this plant wither away by midsummer.

How to start Best done by division in the fall when the plants are fully dormant, although they can also be divided in early spring just as their growth begins. Occasionally offered in seed catalogs, wakerobin seeds require stratification and may take more than two years to germinate and many more years to

Trillium grandiflorum

Trollius europaeus

bloom. Make sure plants have been propagated at a nursery; this plant is unfortunately still collected from the wild in large numbers.

Where to plant   Wakerobin does best in light to deep shade under deciduous trees. The soil should be moist, rich, and slightly acid with plenty of organic matter. Set plants 1 foot apart. Does best in wild gardens where it can be left to grow on its own.

Care   Can be difficult to introduce but spreads moderately once established. Avoid digging or working near this plant when it is dormant during the summer, as its tuberous rootstalks are easily damaged. It's a good idea to put a plant marker nearby to mark its place.

Trollius europaeus
(*Trol*-ee-us)
Common globeflower

Buttercup family; native to Europe and arctic North America
Height: 1 to 3 feet
Spread: 1½ feet
Hardy to zone 3

Globeflowers are leafy, bushy plants that produce rounded, globular blossoms in many shades of yellow and orange. They bloom in late spring and early summer, and are an excellent choice for moist, heavy soil that most other perennials abhor.

Flowers come in many shades of yellow and orange, according to variety. They are 1 to 3 inches across and are composed of 5 to 15 showy sepals in a round, ball that looks as if it has never fully opened. The flowers appear on the ends of long stems in May and June.

The dark green leaves are deeply divided into three to five lobes and have a medium texture. The basal leaves have stalks and are larger and more dense than the stem leaves, whose bottom portions wrap around the stems. The stems grow 1 to 3 feet tall, depending upon variety, and in upright clusters, creating bushy, rounded masses. The foliage is attractive all season.

Globeflowers are long-lived and restrained in growth. The clumps gradually expand by sending up new shoots on the outside perimeter of the crown.

How to start   Planting divisions in late summer is the best method. Plants can also be started from seed that has first been frozen for two days in the freezer and then sown outdoors in late summer. Fresh seed germinates well in six or seven weeks. Old seed may take two years or more to sprout.

Where to plant   Fertile, very moist soil high in organic matter is best, but avoid boggy conditions. Although they prefer partial shade, globeflowers tolerate full sun if the soil is kept moist. Space plants 12 inches apart.

Care   Easy in moist soil. Remove faded flowers to prolong the bloom period. Keep well watered, as these plants must never dry out. They have no serious pests. The plant usually requires division every five years or so to reduce crowding, but if necessary can survive much longer without disturbance. To increase, divide in late summer.

Verbascum olympicum
(Ver-*bas*-kum)
Olympic mullein

Snapdragon family; native to Greece
Height: 5 feet
Spread: 3 feet
Hardy to zone 5

Mullein can almost be considered two plants in one. The first is grown for its broad rosette of basal leaves, which are so heavily covered with hairs as to appear almost snow white in color. The second is a flowering plant with showy, upright, narrow flower spikes. Each bears hundreds of small, bright yellow flowers with woolly white filaments. It blooms in the summer in July and August. Olympic mullein is a biennial or short-lived perennial.

How to start   Easily grown from spring-sown seeds, which yield attractive foliage by midsummer of the first year. Flowering begins the next year.

Where to plant   Native to warm, dry climates, mullein will not tolerate wet, cold soil. It is best grown in full sun in

Verbascum olympicum

Veronica hybrid

light or sandy soil. It looks best in a large border or wild garden.

Care Moderately easy. Cut back the flower stalk after blooming to encourage side branches, which will bloom later in the summer. Cutting back the flower stalk also stimulates the production of offsets in a plant that would normally die after flowering. Mulleins have no serious pests or diseases.

Related species *Verbascum phoenicium* (purple mullein) is very similar to olympic mullein but with purple, red, or pink flowers. 'Mary' is a choice selection of olympic mullein. It is hardy to zone 4.

Veronica hybrids

(Ver-*on*-i-ka)
Speedwell

Snapdragon family; of diverse hybrid origin, the parents are generally native to Europe and Asia
Height: 1 to 2½ feet
Spread: 1 to 1½ feet
Hardy to zone 4

The colorful spikes of speedwell make quite a show in July and August. Many cultivars are available, and most are selected from crosses between *Veronica longifolia* and *V. spicata*. Several other species are also of interest, and they are noted here. (Don't confuse speedwell with the shrub commonly called veronica, which is *Hebe*.)

Speedwell is excellent in the middle of the perennial border, in a clump as a specimen plant, or in the rock garden.

The flowers are usually blue, although varieties are available in pink, purple, and white. Individually they are small and gathered into dense, narrow spikes at the ends of the branches. They bloom in late June through the middle of August.

The light green leaves sometimes have a grayish cast, are lance shaped, and about 2 inches long. Of medium texture, they are held opposite one another on the upright stems. The plant produces bushy clusters of stems that can be either branched or unbranched. Varieties range in size from 12 to 30 inches tall, although most grow to around 18 inches.

Most varieties are long-lived and fairly restrained in growth. The clumps enlarge by sending up many new shoots at the perimeter.

How to start Named varieties should be started by divisions planted in spring or fall. Sow seed outdoors in the spring; there is considerable variation from hybrid seed.

Where to plant The soil should not be too fertile, but it must be well drained. Full sun is best, but the plant tolerates partial shade. Space plants 12 to 18 inches apart.

Care Moderately easy. Speedwell looks best when watered regularly. Removing faded flowers will prolong the bloom season. Downy mildew and leaf spot can be serious problems, especially in humid areas. If these diseases are likely, protect the plants with a fungicide. Division probably is necessary every four years for the best appearance of most varieties. It is an excellent means of increase and can be done either in the spring or fall.

Related species and varieties *Veronica incana* (woolly speedwell) has white, furry leaves on 12- to 18-inch stems. The foliage contrasts well with the pale blue flower spikes in June and July. This plant must have excellent drainage to survive wet winters.

V. latifolia 'Crater Lake Blue', formerly called *V. teucrium*, has bright blue flowers over a long season, nearly all summer. It grows to 18 inches with a tangled, much-branched habit of growth.

V. longifolia (clump speedwell) bears light blue flowers on 12-inch plants from July through August.

V. spicata (spike speedwell) is similar to *V. longifolia*, growing 18 inches tall with many branches. The flower spikes are usually shorter but are very densely produced.

Perennial Sources

The following is a list of suppliers for perennials and seeds. Some of these companies charge for their catalogs; the amount paid for the catalog can usually be applied to any future purchases.

American Daylily & Perennials
Box 210
Grain Valley, MO 64029
816-224-2852; fax 816-443-2849
Specialists in daylilies.

Bluestone Perennials
7211 Middle Ridge Road
Madison, OH 44057
800-852-5243
Specialists in perennials.

Cruickshank's
1015 Mount Pleasant Road
Toronto, Ontario
Canada M4P 2M1
416-488-8292; fax 416-488-8802
*Specialists in flowering bulbs
and perennials.*

Lamb Nurseries
East 101 Sharp Avenue
Spokane, WA 99202

George W. Park Seed Co.
Cokesbury Road
Greenwood, SC 29647-0001

Thompson & Morgan, Inc.
Box 1308
Jackson, NJ 08527
908-363-2225
*Flowering perennial seeds. Represented in Canada by Cruickshank's,
listed above.*

Wayside Gardens
1 Garden Lane
Hodges, SC 29695-0001
800-845-1124
*Flowering perennials. No Canadian
orders.*

White Flower Farm
Route 63, Box 50
Litchfield, CT 06759
800-678-5164

Climate Zone Map

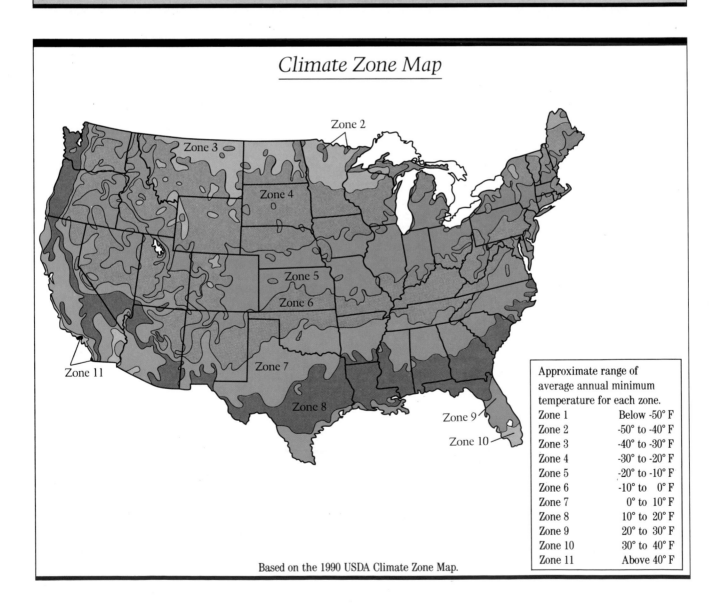

Approximate range of average annual minimum temperature for each zone.	
Zone 1	Below -50° F
Zone 2	-50° to -40° F
Zone 3	-40° to -30° F
Zone 4	-30° to -20° F
Zone 5	-20° to -10° F
Zone 6	-10° to 0° F
Zone 7	0° to 10° F
Zone 8	10° to 20° F
Zone 9	20° to 30° F
Zone 10	30° to 40° F
Zone 11	Above 40° F

Based on the 1990 USDA Climate Zone Map.

INDEX

Note: Page numbers in bold-face type indicate principal references; page numbers in italic type refer to illustrations or photographs.

U.S. Measure and Metric Measure Conversion Chart

		Formulas for Exact Measures			Rounded Measures for Quick Reference		
	Symbol	When you know:	Multiply by:	To find:			
Mass (Weight)	oz	ounces	28.35	grams	1 oz		= 30 g
	lb	pounds	0.45	kilograms	4 oz		= 115 g
	g	grams	0.035	ounces	8 oz		= 225 g
	kg	kilograms	2.2	pounds	16 oz	= 1 lb	= 450 g
					32 oz	= 2 lb	= 900 g
					36 oz	= 2¼ lb	= 1000g (1 kg)
Volume	pt	pints	0.47	liters	1 c	= 8 oz	= 250 ml
	qt	quarts	0.95	liters	2 c (1 pt)	= 16 oz	= 500 ml
	gal	gallons	3.785	liters	4 c (1 qt)	= 32 oz	= 1 liter
	ml	milliliters	0.034	fluid ounces	4 qt (1 gal)	= 128 oz	= 3¾ liter
Length	in.	inches	2.54	centimeters	⅜ in.	= 1 cm	
	ft	feet	30.48	centimeters	1 in.	= 2.5 cm	
	yd	yards	0.9144	meters	2 in.	= 5 cm	
	mi	miles	1.609	kilometers	2½ in.	= 6.5 cm	
	km	kilometers	0.621	miles	12 in. (1 ft)	= 30 cm	
	m	meters	1.094	yards	1 yd	= 90 cm	
	cm	centimeters	0.39	inches	100 ft	= 30 m	
					1 mi	= 1.6 km	
Temperature	°F	Fahrenheit	⅝ (after subtracting 32)	Celsius	32° F	= 0° C	
	°C	Celsius	⅝ (then add 32)	Fahrenheit	212° F	= 100° C	
Area	in.²	square inches	6.452	square centimeters	1 in.²	= 6.5 cm²	
	ft²	square feet	929.0	square centimeters	1 ft²	= 930 cm²	
	yd²	square yards	8361.0	square centimeters	1 yd²	= 8360 cm²	
	a.	acres	0.4047	hectares	1 a.	= 4050 m²	